THE BOOK OF THE POODLE

THE

BOOK

OF

THE

1950

new york

THE VIKING PRESS

POODLE

by

T. H. TRACY

with drawings by Jesse Spicer and Flavia Gág

THIS BOOK

IS DEDICATED TO

MY WIFE

Margaret Ray Tracy

CONTENTS

THE BOOK OF THE POODLE

chapter 1

ORIGIN, HISTORY, AND VARIETIES

The lines are fallen unto me in pleasant places; yea, I have a goodly heritage.

PSALMS 16:6

The Queen sent messengers all over the land to find out his name but none could do so. One night a messenger came back to the castle and although he had not found out the name, upon returning to the castle he passed through some woods and saw a little man jumping up and down singing the following:

"Today I bake; tomorrow I brew my beer;
The next day I will bring the Queen's child here.
Ah! Lucky 'tis that not a soul doth know
That Rumpelstiltskin is my name, Ho! Ho!"

On the third day the little man appeared before the Queen to take her child away and he said to her, "Of course you do not know what my name is." The Queen said, "Rumpelstiltskin," and at this, the little man swore that the Devil must have told her his name.

—GRIMMS' FAIRY TALES

THERE IS A STORY TOLD ABOUT A NEW YORK ACTOR WHO made frequent trips to Chicago, always taking his poodle with him. On one of these excursions the Pullman conductor came into the compartment and discovered the two of them playing cards. Astounded, the man inquired if the poodle really knew how to play cards, and, when assured that he did, exclaimed, "He must be a pretty smart dog if he can play gin rummy."

"Oh, he's not so smart," the actor replied. "I beat him all the time!"

This story Mrs. Milton S. Erlanger of the Pillicoc Kennels, New Jersey, likes to believe is true. However, if the actor's poodle had happened to be her Rumpelstiltskin, he would undoubtedly have beaten his master in nine games out of ten. The history of this most unusual dog is, in a way, the history of the poodle in the United States.

Rumpelstiltskin's father was Ch. Cadeau de Noel, a handsome brown standard acquired by Mrs. Erlanger through Mrs. Whitehouse Walker, who found the dog in England as a puppy. At that time (1931) brown poodles were not in great demand, but Mrs. Walker, sensing his great possibilities, thought it would be unfair not to exhibit him. She did so, and he achieved his championship and obedience title in a very short time.

In his private life he was known as Caddy. Although he was the first dog to win a CDX (Companion Dog Excellent) title in obedience trial work sponsored by the American Kennel Club—winning at White Plains, New York, in 1936 over imported champions—he had the whimsical personality of a clown. He loved to dance, and at Saturday night reunions at the Erlanger estate he would actually cut in on a dance with Mrs. Erlanger.

With the innate subtlety of his breed Caddy made a point of getting away with just so much and no more, depending upon whoever happened to be involved, and he would size up a person thoroughly before going to work on him. For example, he considered Mr. Erlanger a softie, and got away with murder in consequence, but he paid strict attention to the commands of Henry Stoecker, trainer and handler of the Pillicoc Kennels. Stoecker held the opinion that Caddy was the most perfect of fools, and he always pointed out that the court jesters of old imparted wisdom and learning to their kings.

Mrs. Erlanger had always wanted to give Henry Stoecker a poodle puppy to train and show, and as litter after litter arrived in the kennels, puppies were offered to him but were consistently refused. In the early months of 1935 a mating was arranged between Caddy and Ch. Giroflee of Misty Isles, a sloe-eyed black siren owned by Thomas Frelinghuysen, neighbor of the Erlangers. The whelping took place on May 30, 1935.

It had been predetermined by the most scientific methods available that there would be five puppies, and names had been chosen for them. When a sixth puppy made its appearance Mr. Frelinghuysen, somewhat disconcerted, telephoned Mrs. Erlanger to insist that a name be found immediately for the unexpected arrival. "A name? Must I guess? Why, that's easy," Mrs. Erlanger replied. "Call him Rumpelstiltskin!"

Henry Stoecker followed the development of the black litter closely, concentrating on Rumpelstiltskin from the start. Then, when the puppy was three months old, he announced, "This is it!" and proceeded to tell Mrs. Erlanger that since he had been offered the choice of a pup, this was the one he wanted. He took the little fellow home, called him Curly, and at once began his training, with the result that at the age of seven and a half months Rumpelstiltskin won reserve winners at Madison Square Garden, and before he was a year old obtained his championship.

He did more; he popularized the breed in the United States as no other poodle has ever done.

Indeed, Rumpelstiltskin, or Curly, could do just about everything. When a visitor came to the Stoecker house he would be met at the door by the poodle, who would politely take his hat and hang it on a peg. Next the visitor's gloves would be carried off with enthusiasm and deposited on the hall stand.

Curly was a super house dog. He learned to pick up the dishes from the dining-room table, carry them to the kitchen, and place them on the drainboard. But Henry Stoecker says that perhaps Curly's greatest domestic achievement was his ability to carry half a cup of black coffee from the breakfast nook to the kitchen without spilling a drop.

Out of doors Curly was an exuberant hunter on his own. He killed snakes, rats, and woodchucks; he retrieved ducks, logs, and orange crates from the seashore. He was also a trained hunter, learning to "fetch" and to "freeze" like a setter or pointer. He could balance himself with all four feet on an upended beer mug. Powerful, well-coupled, and weighing about sixty-eight pounds, he was also attack-trained.

His leisure moments were spent in his favorite spot, beneath an apple tree in the Stoecker yard, watching the world go by with eyes like black diamonds. Henry Stoecker declares that Curly was never sick until the afternoon a few green apples dropped while he was meditating under the apple tree. Curly, being of a curious nature, tried a couple of bites. The resulting green-apple cake walk gave Mr. Stoecker an anxious two hours, but Curly never picked up anything strange after that, with the exception of four bananas, which he devoured skin and all. Of course he would try anything his master ate, and on occasions when Stoecker gave him a pickle, mustard, or a persimmon, the dog would eat it and then look up at him as if to say, "Boy, you must have a cast-iron stomach if you're able to digest stuff like that!"

Frequently week-end guests at the Erlanger home were entertained by Curly being blindfolded and locked in an adjoining room while somebody was given a pack of playing cards and asked to pick one out. The card having been replaced and the deck shuffled and spread out on the floor, Curly would be called in and told to find the chosen card—which he invariably did.

Here is another incident that demonstrates the sagacity and hereditary courage of this prince of dogs. At the top of the Erlanger Jersey house was a "widow-walk," somewhat similar to those of Nantucket. The only access to it was by means of a ladder from the attic, and the first time Curly went up he climbed it like an old salt going topside to hoist a sail. The height was ten feet or more to the roof, and Mrs. Erlanger held her breath, wondering how Curly would ever get down, but Stoecker assured her that he would—the same way he got up. And, sure enough, this spectacular dog calmly descended the ladder without the slightest difficulty.

Obedience work was pie to him, and he won his title in an amazingly short time. He could jump an eight-foot fence and also leap backward over an ordinary hurdle. In 1936 he traveled through most of the United States with Henry Stoecker, who handled him in the ring. He romped off with top honors to such an extent that in 1937 he received the Annual Award of the American Kennel Club for the best American-bred dog of all breeds.

There is no doubt that Curly had a sense of premonition. Somehow he seemed to know when he was going to win, whether in a group or best in show. When he was due for a success he would start to wag his tail as the judge walked toward the table to enter his final decision. Stoecker says that Curly never failed in this signal. When he wagged his tail he won, and when he didn't there was no top honor. The tail-wagging was not the furious wag of a young novice, but a slow metronomic oscillation that said calmly, "Don't worry, Henry. We're in!" Furthermore, he always insisted on taking his ribbon from the judge and stood up on his hind legs to receive it.

One instance of his clairvoyance has gone down in dog-show history. At the Morris and Essex Show in 1937 he had the greatest competition of his career. A black chow-chow, Ch. Farland Thunder-gust, was acclaimed by everybody as the certain best in show, and finally the decision rested between Curly and the chow. The air was electric as the judge turned his back to get the blue ribbon. Suddenly Curly started to wag his tail. Stoecker, who was positive that the chow would be the winner, leaned over to him and whispered, "You're wrong this time, boy. The chow is sure to get it." But Curly, as usual, was right.

The following summer the poodle and his trainer were at the annual Wilkes-Barre, Pennsylvania, show, and the temperature was over 100 degrees. The heat was taking its toll; the dogs were listless and panting, and even Curly didn't appear to feel right. Stoecker took his temperature and found it to be 104, but decided to go through with the show as Curly had won best of variety and was soon due in the ring with eight other winners to compete for the best in the non-sporting group. Entering the ring for this semifinal, Stoecker tightened the lead and told him, "Pull yourself together, Curly, we've got to do our best." He says that he felt the dog stiffen proudly and step forward with the style that was born in him, the inimitable class that had made him famous. The judging took only a few minutes and Curly won. The best! But as they left the ring he sagged, and in his crate wilted and became limp. Stoecker went back to congratulate the judge on the fastest group work he had ever seen, and the judge said, "Why not? Your dog was the only one that had the class. The others were like a lot of wet rags."

Following the Wilkes-Barre Show came the southern circuit. Stoecker wound up one night in Tennessee in a town where the only two good hotels were filled, so he went to one on a side street and asked for a room. The price was two dollars. He was requested to pay in advance, which he did with a two-dollar bill, and started toward the elevator with Curly. As he neared it the clerk called him back to the desk, saying that it was a rule of the hotel to allow no dogs. The man had not yet rung up the money; it was lying on the counter. Stoecker, agreeing that he didn't want any rules broken either, told Curly, "Fetch!" The dog immediately jumped up on the counter and retrieved the two-dollar bill.

In spite of these amazing proofs of an almost human intelligence, the champion had one eccentric little habit that endeared him to his fans, but not to his photographers. Of course, he had been photographed literally hundreds of times in show rings and may have become a little bored with it. When a photographer, after taking a picture, put his camera on the floor in order to take notes, Curly would promptly march over to it and lift his leg. Henry Stoecker thinks that this was a manifestation of the ham in him, but Mrs. Erlanger feels that he was just saying, "Boo to you!" Students of inherited traits may be interested in knowing that Caddy, Curly's father, performed the same function on his dumbbell after he had finished with it in an obedience class.

L'Envoi: Curly spent the latter part of his life relaxing under his favorite apple tree and serving as a stud dog for a one-hundred-and-fifty-dollar fee. Probably no poodle ever sired more champions than Curly.

There came a night in October 1948 when, after he had finished his usual sturdy dinner, he went out for a short walk. He returned a few minutes later and, although not complaining, evidenced that his rheumatism was getting the better of him. He didn't die, they say, he was just too tired to get up. He was buried under the beloved apple tree.

The story of Rumpelstiltskin will live on and be told as long as poodle owners gather together and brag about their breed. But all the legends and the history of the poodle strain stir the imagination. Get more than one poodle fancier in a room, bring up the word "origin," and you have a king-sized argument on your hands. There are probably more theories, genetic guesses, and wild fancies told about the origin and background of these dogs than there are owners. Many of the strains officially recognized today as purebreds are the result of purposeful and clever cross-breeding, but in the case of the poodle it is difficult, in view of what we know, to deny its ancient puristic origin. If poodles were the result of cross-breeding, their ancestry definitely would be traceable and there could be little argument about it.

The breed was first heard of in northern Germany and western Russia in the sixteenth century. Gesner, circa 1553, mentions the *pudel*, and it was known in Russia by the same name; the word connotes "splashing in water." In those days the poodle was utilized as a sporting dog, specifically a water retriever or fowl dog, and in that capacity he had no superior. He was a large dog similar to the standard poodles of today, and his color was usually black, except in Germany, where it was more frequently brown. He was known in Belgium and Holland as a *poedel* and used chiefly as a working dog. Dürer

Ch. Cadeau de Noel, sire of Ch. Rumpelstiltskin,
in one of his prancing moods

photos by Tauskey

Ch. Rumpelstiltskin

Early bronze, probably English,
from the collection of B. Ormond Riblett

Poodle figurine made in Bennington, Vermont, circa 1850

During the reign of Louis Philippe (1830–1848) a tax was imposed on dogs in France. Many dogs whose owners attempted tax evasion were impounded, and legend has it that a poodle found a means of escape and led the dogs to freedom. This lithograph, printed during this period, shows a housewife attempting (unsuccessfully, perhaps) to convince the collector that she should be exempt from the tax. She argues, "Azor is indispensable for guarding the home, while Finette is indispensable to Azor, and besides he is company. Turk is a foreigner, not naturalized, and therefore should not pay any tax. The poodle is not useful, therefore I think we are tax free, don't you?"

"Innocent Amusements," an etching by Theodore Lane, London, 1827

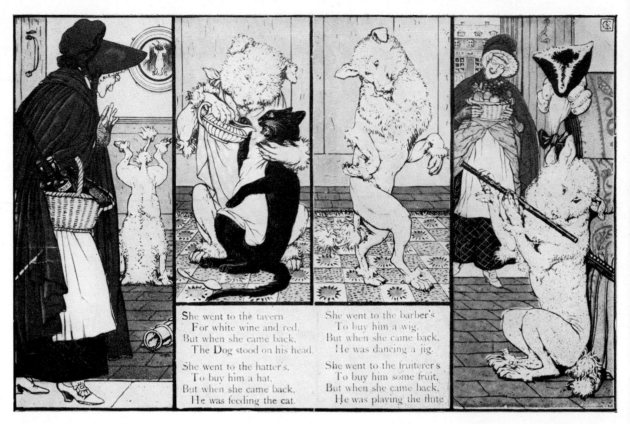

She went to the tavern
For white wine and red.
But when she came back,
The Dog stood on his head.

She went to the hatter's.
To buy him a hat.
But when she came back,
He was feeding the cat.

She went to the barber's
To buy him a wig,
But when she came back,
He was dancing a jig.

She went to the fruiterer's
To buy him some fruit,
But when she came back,
He was playing the flute.

From *Old Mother Hubbard,* as illustrated by Walter Crane, circa 1880

"Behind the Scenes," by Ludwig Knaus (1880), foremost German genre painter

"Clown with Horse," by Henri de Toulouse-Lautrec

Toy poodle, with ribbon in hair, being served a leg of chicken.
Print by Le Bon Genre, Paris, 1818.

Munito, favorite poodle of Paris, giving one of his performances.
Print by Le Bon Genre, Paris, 1817.

executed a painting in 1510 which is unmistakably that of a poodle, while about the same time Caspar of Bohemia did a small painting on wood of a bearded personage in a befurred pelisse accompanied by a poodle.

Gradually the breed migrated westward to France, where it was utilized for fowling and known only as a *barbet*, which literally meant "beard" but was extended colloquially to denote a long-haired dog. There was no scientific classification in these early times, although around 1570 John Kay wrote a pamphlet in Latin having to do with "English dogges." A loose translation of this was undertaken by Abraham Fleming and published in England in 1576. It represents, as far as we know, the first attempt at classifying dogs, and it is noteworthy that many were classified according to function. For example:

Tumblers	*Butcher's Dogge*
Stealers	*The Shepherd's Dogge*
Land Spaniels	*Carrier*
Setters	*Tynker's Cure*
Water Spaniels	*The Mooner.*
Spaniel Gentle or Comforter	*The Village Dogge or Housekeeper*
Mongrel and Rascall Sort	*Daunser*
Wapp or Warner	

The pamphlet mentions a dog whose service is required upon the water. "This sort is somewhat bigge and of measurable greatnesse, having long, rough and curled heare . . . powled and notted from the shoulders to the hindermost legges and to the end of his tayle."

The author characterized these dogs as Aquaticus because of their natural love of water, and he also mentioned the necessity of shearing them in order to give them more swiftness and lightness in swimming. They became known in England in the seventeenth century as waterdogs, and the difference of opinion as to whether the poodle is identical with the water-dog, or a descendant of the water-dog, has long been argued. But the poodle was known as the poodle before there was a water-dog classification in England, and their identities merged in the early part of the nineteenth century when the waterdog became known as the poodle and the former name or classification became extinct.

In 1621 Gervase Markham, English writer on veterinary matters, said in *The Whole Arte of Fowling by Water and Land:* "Your dog may be of any color and yet excellent, and his hair in general would be long and curled, not loose and shagged; for the first shows hardness and ability to endure the water, the other much tenderness and weakness, making his sport grievous; his head would be round and curled, his ears broad and hanging, his eye full, lively and quick, his nose very short, his lip hound-like, side and rough bearded, his choppes with a full set of strong teeth and the general features of his whole countenance being united together would be as lion like as might be, for that shows fierceness and goodness; his neck would be thick and short, his breast like the breast of a ship, sharp and compact, his shoulders broad, his forelegs straight, his chin square, his buttocks round, his ribs compact, his belly gaunt, his thighs brawny, his cambrels crooked, his pasterns strong and dew-clawed, and all his four feet spacious, full and round, and closed together to the cley, like a water duck, for they being his oars to row him in the water, having that shape, will carry his body away the faster." The similarity of this description to that of the ideal poodle is most striking.

The poodle was known in England as early as 1636. Prince Rupert of the Palatinate went to England that year to aid Charles I in his war with the Roundheads and brought with him his poodle named Boy. Van Dyck was commissioned to paint them both. In 1643 there was printed in London a pamphlet entitled *Observations upon Prince Ruppert's White Dogge Called Boye*. (An original is in the possession of Mrs. L. W. Bonney, Tally-Ho Kennels, Oyster Bay, New York.)

The pamphlet is a "dialogue, or rather a parley betweene Prince Ruppert's Dogge whose name is Puddle, and Tobie's Dogge whose name is Pepper, etc.," and the two dogs argue over the respective merits of the Cavaliers and the Roundheads. Pepper asks Boy if he is an ordinary dog, and he replies, "No sirrah, I am of a high german breed." The frontispiece contains an excellent woodcut engraving showing a group of Cavaliers on the left, headed by Prince Rupert and Boy, challenging a group of Roundheads. The Prince is sicking Boy onto the Roundheads and saying, "To him Pudel."

Boy was reported to speak many languages, to be invulnerable in battle, and able to put a hex on the enemy. He died at the battle of Marston Moors in 1644, and it is a matter of historical record that all witches, sorcerers, the Pope, and the Devil were invited to mourn at his funeral.

In the mid-eighteenth century the Swedish naturalist Linnaeus classified dogs as follows:

Canis Domesticus	Domesticated dog
Canis Sagax	Wise dog
Canis Graius	Greyhound
Canis Mastinus	A great dog
Canis Aquaticus	Water-dog
Canis Militacus	Pet dog
Canis Aegyptius	Egyptian dog
Canis Fricatrix	Russian dog or cold dog
Canis Mustelinus	Weasel or weasle-coloured dog

Here, perhaps for the first time, is found the water-dog classification, embracing, perforce, poodles and other types that functioned in the water.

Around 1792, in an English work *The Animal Kingdom*, dogs were classified in thirty-six breeds. Included in the breeds were Canis Aquaticus Major, called a great water-dog—"The hair is long and curled, like the fleece of a sheep"; Canis Aquaticus Minor, the lesser water-dog, which was "of a small size, with long curly hair, which about the ears is longer and hangs downwards"; and Canis Leoninus, the lion-dog, which "is exceedingly small, with long hair, like the foregoing, on the forepart of the body; that on the hindparts being shorter and smooth."

Here exists, for the first time in England, a classification of the poodle in two varieties, or possibly three, if the lion-dog is included. The Germans already had their pudels classified in four sizes: great, medium, little, and pinsch. It may very well be that the lion-dog classification was the miniature or toy poodle. This lion-dog should not be confused with the lion-dog that appeared in the Mediterranean countries sometime later, and soon thereafter became extinct. The failure to distinguish between the two led one writer, as late as 1927, to imply that the poodle was descended from the Mediterranean lion-dog. One early writer described the Mediterranean lion-dog as a cross between a barbet and a naked Turk and of no consequence whatsoever. The poodle's heavy, woolly coat dispels any idea that the breed originated in the Mediterranean region.

In 1790, Ralph Beilby published his *General History of Quadrupeds* in which he mentioned the rough water-dog, used for hunting ducks, "taking up birds . . . that drop into the sea," a smaller variety of the water-dog, and a lion-dog with "head and forepart of body covered with shaggy hair . . . hinder part smooth, a tuft of hair at the end of tail."

Around 1840 W. C. L. Martin, English scientist, attempted to classify dogs according to ears and muzzle. He placed the poodle in the following classification: "Ears, moderately large, sometimes very large, pendent; hair, long and fine; muzzle moderate; forehead, developed; scent, acute; intelligence at a high ratio."

A short time later, in 1853, Professor David Low of the University of Edinburgh classified all dogs, in his book *Domesticated Animals*, into four groups. One was known as the Indagator Group, and in this he placed the poodle as "a dog of aquatic situations. His feet are webbed, and he swims and dives with rapidity and ease."

Although the French claimed the caniche, or poodle, as their very own and will always do so, there exists no proof for its French origin as compared to the evidence of its German origin. M. de Buffon, in his *Natural History* published in 1755, mentions the grand barbet and the petit barbet; their descriptions are identical with those of the water-dog of England and the pudel of Germany. The *Dictionnaire des Sciences*, 1751-1780, which Diderot helped to edit, does not mention the caniche. It does mention the barbet as a "vigorous, intelligent, sturdy, curly-haired dog that goes into the water." The *Dictionnaire Moreri*, published in 1759, does not mention the caniche, nor does it mention the barbet. *Nouveau Larousse*, 1864-1876, mentions the caniche as a "barbet type." Spiers and Surenne's Dictionary, 1852, defines the caniche as a "poodle dog or water-dog," and *E. Littre Dictionnaire* of 1878 defines the poodle as a "barbet dog." It also defines the barbet as a dog with long curly hair.

Some French writers have claimed that the caniche, or poodle, descended from the barbet, but without giving any enlightenment on or scientific classification of the barbet. It would appear that barbet was a term used to describe any type or breed of dog with the characteristic of excessive hair. Of course the poodle had already endeared himself to the French. Even today, there are many persons who erroneously call the breed "French poodle." In France a common expression is "loyal as a poodle."

In England the first reference to the water-dog as a poodle was made in *The Sportsman's Repository*, published in 1820. William Youatt followed suit in 1847 and claimed the water-dog was a poodle, but Hugh Dalziel, in his book *British Dogs* published in 1870, said there was no resemblance between the water-dog and the poodle, although photographs appear to contradict this successfully. Colonel Charles H. Smith, the well-known naturalist, insisted that the dog known as the water-dog was a poodle. In the *Naturalist's Library*, published in Edinburgh in 1840, he wrote that the water-dog was the poodle of the Germans—the barbet of the Continent. James Dickie in *The Dog* entered the argument and observed that the water-dog was none other than the poodle, and Robert Leighton, author of *Book of the Dog*, anxiously observed that he felt that the poodle was closely related to the water-dog. Rawdon E. Lee, whose word was apparently final, said in his *Modern Dogs* (1899) that the water-dog was definitely a poodle and a "very distinct variety of dog," at no time crossed with any other type of English dog. Sir William Jardine, in his all-inclusive *Naturalist's Library*, said definitely that the poodle was of German origin, and Hubbard in his *The Observer's Book of Dogs* also said that the poodle originated in Germany and existed there for centuries, being used as a water-fowl dog and sheep herder.

As early as 1700 the French discovered the natural performing and acting ability of their barbet or caniche. Lee pointed out that in 1700 a troupe of poodles from France danced in London. They were probably called Performing Dogs or Dancers. Hubbard noted that around 1780 the miniature poodle was in favor as the French pet. He also mentioned that the toy poodle must have been in fashion around 1490, since the Italian artist Pinturiccio showed one. He also claimed that Alexander Pope's dog Bounce was a poodle. Others believed that Merrylegs in Dickens' *Hard Times* was a poodle. Certainly both names are apropos in the joie de vivre they express.

Typical of these performing dogs were those of Signor M. Girmondi, who, after performing before the crowned heads of Europe at Berlin, Paris, Vienna, and Madrid, came to England and played before King George III, "also before Her Majesty and the whole of the Royal Family at Windsor Castle on Tuesday, November 5, 1815," after which he toured England. These dogs pushed a wheelbarrow, danced, jumped through hoops, skipped rope, operated a spinning wheel, tumbled, marched in a funeral procession, and did many other tricks. A combination advertisement, advance sheet, and program, published at Manchester, England, in 1817, describes and illustrates the acts and states: "Their years are young but their experience old; and this description paints their tricks, which far transcend the power of pen to give. One scene is that of two dogs coming on stage bearing a sedan-chair in which is seated a tumbler who though not more than two months old is an adept on ground and lofty exploits. This scene peculiarly claims the attention of the audience. After finishing the tumbling he is carried off in the same vehicle. This young tumbler is a small French Poodle of great sagacity and quick apprehension, capable of being instructed in most tricks and receives his lessons with attention, particularly from one month old and upwards."

Goethe, in 1780, depicted Mephistopheles as coming to earth in the form of a black poodle. Faust and Wagner first see the animal as they are going to the city. Faust: "Inspect him close; for what takest thou the beast?" Wagner: "Why, for a pudel who has lost his master. . . . Naught but a plain black pudel do I see."

In Paris, in 1814, a poodle named Munito reigned as a stage star. Munito could play dominoes, do arithmetic, and perform baffling card tricks. But the pièce de résistance was the act in which a name or word was written on a blackboard; Munito would then spell out the word by choosing alphabetical blocks.

The popularization of the poodle in England began shortly after 1800. English soldiers, engaged in the Napoleonic Wars on the Continent, became enamored of the pudel of Germany and the caniche of France. The French word caniche is derived from the word *canard*, indicating that the French made considerable use of the breed for duck-retrieving. The English soldiers found that a poodle served as mascot to practically every French regiment and were completely won over by its animated, sparkling qualities, which were not found in the stolid English types. They brought home as many poodles as they could.

Around 1820 the craftsmen of Rockingham began to turn out the exquisite poodle figurines which are so much in demand today. But the English were not quite won over. One commentator, observing poodles performing as dancers and tumblers, wrote that the poodle was considered a mere trick dog and a companion to mountebanks. But Dalziel attributed high intelligence to the poodle and felt it should have a destiny higher than "a buffoon of the canine race, merely to pander to a frivolous taste." The adoption of the poodle into fashionable society could hardly be considered his fault, since the English did not utilize his natural ability to retrieve in fowl shooting. They preferred their own breeds. Also, the English marshes were being drained around this period and water fowl were scarce.

T. Heath Joyce, English sportsman, was among the first ardent supporters of the poodle in England. He complained that the poodle was not understood and appreciated there, "and yet in a great measure those very characteristics which render him first and foremost among canine performers are due to the simple fact that he is far superior in intelligence to his fellows, and capable of acquiring a greater variety of accomplishments, from walking about on his hind-legs with a parasol and petticoats, to retrieving on land or water."

But the poodle was not be denied. In 1840 Colonel Charles H. Smith said the poodle "was occasionally also brought to the environs of London in order to afford the brutal sport of hunting and worrying to death domestic ducks placed in ponds for that purpose." At Lambeth there was a public inn known as The Dog and Duck, where patrons were entertained by ducks being thrown into an enclosed pond and the poodles diving after them. Another writer noted: "Within the last few years, a good many poodles have been imported into England for wild-fowl shooting, but a still greater number have been introduced as ladies' pets, the fashion of the day being in favour of a poodle with a black satin jacket trimmed with Astrakhan." Gradually the poodle was taken away from the water, his natural habitat, and Frank T. Barton remarked: "The poodle still maintains its position as a companion to the wealthy; indeed, one may take it as fair evidence that the proprietor of a well-groomed and fashionably clipped poodle is a person of affluent circumstances. There is, as it were, the hallmark of aristocracy upon a typical specimen of this breed."

In 1840 Landseer, the renowned English animal painter, recognizing the sapience of the poodle, painted his famous "Laying Down the Law," a copy of which will be found in the home of practically every poodle breeder. The painting shows a judiciously benign-looking white standard poodle giving a legal lecture to dogs of other breeds, apparently on the folly of their repeated transgressions. On the Continent, Toulouse-Lautrec immortalized in drawing the circus poodle of France, a black, tufty animal with curiously angular haunches and a street-Arab expression.

In 1848 there was published in London *A Collection of Anecdotes* by C. De Moor which contains a story of a poodle named Sharges and relates how he swam the Danube and the Rhine. The book also mentions that the dog is a poodle in England, a pudel in Germany, and a caniche or barbet in France. And after 1880 English schoolchildren learned their Old Mother Hubbard in a book with colored drawings by Walter Crane, who portrayed Mother Hubbard's dog as a white standard.

The poodles exhibited in England and France during the latter part of the nineteenth century were usually classified in two types, curly and corded. These classifications had to do only with the treatment given the coat. The coat of the curly poodle was similar to that of the poodle of today: it was brushed out evenly. The corded type of coat probably had its genesis in human laxity because brushing was eliminated and the hair allowed to grow without limit, which resulted in an appearance of cultivated, comical sloppiness.

The writings of this period fail to reflect any accurate knowledge about the trichological peculiarities of the poodle. Its hair grows, and if allowed to grow unchecked without grooming or clipping, it will intertwist and form cords. Some fanciers adopted the notion that this was the natural coat of the poodle and began separating the cords into even strands and soaking the coat with oils and ointments to produce an even tighter twist to the cords. The cords of poodles of the time reached the floor, and the weight of the coat must have been excessive. This type of coat has been outmoded for many years as lacking in magnificence and splendor, and also because it is universally recognized that the coat should be brushed.

The poodle first appeared in the Kennel Club stud book in England in 1875, when fair specimens were exhibited at Nottingham. In 1886 the Poodle Club of England was formed, and the following year a corded type of poodle won best in show at the Kennel Club show in London.

In 1887 the first poodle was registered with the American Kennel Club, Inc. The dog, whelped June 14, 1886, by Boy out of Queen, was named Czar. He was owned and imported by W. Lyman Biddle of Philadelphia, whose sister, Mrs. Arthur Biddle, remembers Czar well. She says Czar had a gorgeous black coat, and periodically an expert came down from New York to clip and groom him. However, she found him to be an impossible walking companion because of his predilection for lake water and his ungallant habit of getting caught in the brambles. Evidently the table manners of poodles have not changed, for she recalls that Czar always wore a rubber bib at dinner.

Poodles were exhibited in the United States for some time prior to 1887. The first show where poodles were exhibited under American

Kennel Club rules was in Boston, Massachusetts, in March 1878. Eight poodles were entered in this show; curiously enough, there were more poodles than bulldogs, dachshunds, clumber spaniels, or other breeds presumably more popular at that period. The catalogue lists some of them as follows: "Dot—white–4 years–bred Lima, Peru"; "Poogey—white–French descent," who was for sale at twenty dollars; "Pompey—white–Spanish"; and "Topsey—white and fawn–French poodle."

Well-known writers and fanciers of other breeds have made an honest appraisal of the intellectual capacity of the poodle. If you want it objectively, here it is:

Poodles are, without doubt, the cleverest of dogs.

A. CRAVEN, *Dogs of the World*

The breed is no nincompoop, being extraordinarily intelligent and standing no nonsense from anyone.

HUBBARD, *The Observer's Book of Dogs*

The cerebral cavity is more capacious than in other dogs and the frontal sinuses are fully developed and the general formation of the head and skull exhibit every indication of extraordinary intelligence.

RAWDON E. LEE, *Modern Dogs*

No more distinctive or intelligent variety of domestic dog exists than the poodle, whether in its large or miniature form—a statement which, in my opinion, needs no qualification. Taken as a whole, poodles may be credited with possessing an even temperament, are very affectionate and extremely teachable. Indeed, so far as learning tricks are concerned, it is safe to say that they excell all other varieties.

J. MAXTEE, *Popular Toy Dogs*

The poodle is commonly acknowledged to be the most wisely intelligent of all members of the canine race. He is a scholar and a gentleman. . . . His qualities of mind and his acute powers of reasoning are indeed so great that there is something almost human in his devotion. He is an adept at performing tricks, but it is his alertness of brain that places him apart from other animals.

ROBERT LEIGHTON, *Book of the Dog*

His liveliness, attachment and faithfulness, combined with his good temper, trust and obedience, make of him a thoroughly good companion. He grasps everything he is taught so readily that he is trained very quickly. There is no more sagacious dog than the poodle, none more persevering in his work, none more affectionate to his master; and the true lines of his body are simply as perfect as can be.

J. H. WALSH, *Dogs of the British Isles*

No dog surpasses the poodle in intelligence; in fact, no dog is his equal. . . . He has a quality of mind that borders on the human; his reasoning powers are evident to all with whom he is associated, and there is apparently no limit to his aptitude for learning.

WILLIAM A. BRUETTE, *The Complete Dog Book*

These are very clever, sagacious dogs and there is nothing within reason they cannot be taught.

MRS. DESALIS, *Work on Dogs*

One of the most intelligent breeds in existence. . . . All who have kept any of them will know they are full of merit, good tempered as a rule, born humourists, fond of children, grand swimmers, excellent guards and very affectionate and faithful to their owners and friends.

CHARLES H. LANE, *All About Dogs*

A poodle can do everything but speak, and sometimes even tries that.

GORDON STABLES, *Our Friend the Dog*

He can learn to do almost anything, for he is, possibly, the cleverest alive.

JAMES DICKIE, *The Dog*

The dog, when he's well educated, is by the wisest tolerated. Yes, he deserves your favor thoroughly—the clever scholar of the students, he!

GOETHE, *Faust*

From its peculiar sagacity, it is capable of being trained to almost any useful purpose, and its strong individual attachment renders it more the companion of a man.

WILLIAM YOUATT, *The Dog*

In the United States there are three varieties of the poodle: standard, miniature, and toy.

STANDARD   A purebred poodle that measures 15 inches or over at the shoulder. Exhibited in the non-sporting group.

MINIATURE   A purebred poodle that measures over 10 inches, and under 15, at the shoulder. Exhibited in the non-sporting group.

TOY   A purebred poodle that measures 10 inches and under at the shoulder. Exhibited in the toy group.

The English have only two classifications: The standard, measuring 15 inches and over, and the miniature, measuring under 15 inches, both exhibited in the non-sporting classes. In Germany all poodles are shown in the group known as "utility and pets," while Sweden has the standard, miniature, and toy classifications. In France poodles are shown in the "pet" group, and there are three varieties: the dwarf, less than 13.77 inches; the moyen, from 13.77 inches to 17.71 inches; and the standard, from 17.71 inches to 23.62 inches. There are further subdivisions in accordance with type of coat. In the United States there has been some movement in recent years to create a fourth class, probably called the "medium," and similar to the moyen type that predominates in France. However, this might be inadvisable as it would produce in the long run nothing more than a catch-all or wastebasket variety—in other words, a variety that would contain large miniatures and small standards. This kind of thing often gives scope to unethical breeders; at one time a similar question about color led to the presentation in the ring of Madison Square Garden of particolored toys with nondescript clips and obscure antecedents.

Where did all these classic varieties come from? Originally the poodle of eastern Germany and western Russia, usually black in color, was a large and sturdy dog, yet statuesque, as was the water-dog poodle of England and the grand barbet of France. As he migrated westward in Germany he became slightly smaller, with shorter legs and body, and a few strains developed with thick skulls and short, stubby snouts. These were called "Kraut-heads," and infrequently we see some of them today. The Germans developed the whites and exalted them for a while above other colors. In 1880 the German experts reported that browns were "considered bad." Around this time the Germans were not using the poodle to any great extent as a water-fowl retriever; hunting activities were being transferred to land, and dachshunds were used for hunting badgers, rabbits, and the like. In this same period the Germans were engaged in a tremendous scientific breeding program which later resulted in the production of the boxer, the Doberman pinscher, and other developed species. Breeders in Switzerland took up the breeding of white poodles, and the resplendent white standards of today had their genesis in Swiss kennels. As westward migration proceeded into France, the poodle became smaller and was known as caniche moyen—middle-sized poodle—while the large standard was called, and is today, caniche royale—king size.

Different sizes have existed for over two hundred years, and it is probably true that the miniature is the result of interbreeding between small standards. E. Otto von Bensheim, famed German dog writer, wrote in *German Dogs* that the miniatures "are little wonders." He solemnly stated that they came from heaven in the form of two black clouds which the gods tousled considerably and sent down to earth with a sign on each, reading, "Shave, please," and that they came to rest in a kennel in Baden-Baden.

The toys have existed for almost as many years as the other varieties and are undoubtedly the result of breeding between small miniatures. The first toy registered in the United States was in 1901—one Prince of Bellwood, owned by W. P. Palmer of Chicago. There is no historical justification for the belief that the registered toys are the consequence of a crossing with the Maltese terrier. Never have the toys been in such favor as today, but the true type is still scarce because of the limited number of prepotent sires and dams. Most of the toys are white or cream-colored. There are a few grays and blacks but no browns. Heretofore, breeding has been necessarily restricted to line, and inbreeding and some faulty recessive characteristics have cropped out, but now outcrossing between miniature strains is producing some really excellent specimens, including many good honest blacks. Black being the dominant color, it is essential that pure, typey, and attractive blacks be secured, by inbreeding if possible, to pave the way for structural betterment and expansion of color possibilities.

The poodle's gain in popularity in the United States has been swift and certain in recent years. In 1944 there were but 411 poodles registered with the American Kennel Club. In 1946 there were registrations for 1186 poodles, and the breed stood twenty-fifth in popularity. In 1948 there were 1664 registrations, and the poodle reached twenty-first place. For 1949 there were 2165 registrations, and the poodle jumped to eighteenth place. These figures, it must be remembered, represent only the number of registrations within the particular years. For the first six months of 1950 registrations numbered 1483, presaging a gain of at least twenty-five per cent over 1949.

The poodle's versatility as a watch dog, retriever, and gay companion, his superior intelligence coupled with his emotional stability and physical soundness, assure him of a welcome place in our society. His charm and his desire to please are fundamental attributes. The instinctive qualities of complete fidelity and devotion are known to all. His eagerness for affection is not based upon ambition but on an appeal to the universal heart of mankind; those that live to please must please to live.

Besides, in what other breed can you find a dog that comes in three different sizes and six different colors?

chapter 2

BUYING A PUPPY

To man he looks in all necessities, with speaking eye for assistance; exerts for him all the little services in his power with cheerfulness and pleasure; for him bears famine and fatigue with patience and resignation; no injuries can abate his fidelity, no distress induce him to forsake his benefactor; studious to please and fearing to offend, he is still a humble steadfast dependent; and in him alone fawning is not flattery.

GOLDSMITH: "ON MAD DOGS"

HAVE YOU EVER PLAYED THE FASCINATING GAME OF studying human personalities with the idea of guessing just what breed of dog they own or favor? It is not too difficult. The tweedy type will have a beagle, a setter, or a Chesapeake Bay. The reserved and unassuming will probably go for Dalmatians, while the average dog-loving American, whether of the indoor or outdoor species, will often prefer the American cocker spaniel. The booming, aggressive sort is positive that the boxer is the only dog in the world, whereas a Pekingese can usually be found in the boudoir of one both dainty and exotic, and, although it seems incongruous, the large bosomy type will invariably be found chucking a toy under the chin. A classic sight in almost every dog show is the corpulent dowager with battle in her eye, lumbering into the ring to exhibit a miniscule Chihuahua with thyroid trouble and a rhinestone collar. In fact, there is no better spot for trying your guessing game than the average dog show. There doggy people are known only in relation to their pets. "Oh, that's Miss Smith—she's an Airedale woman," or, "Just look at that nasty little whippett man winning again!"

It is a two-sided game; if you want to know something about the habits, character, and debilities of a person, take a look at his dog. The dog is the alter ego of its owner. The pugnacious dog will have an argumentative master. A sloppy, careless dog indicates that the owner is the same. A growler and croaker will never be found in the company of a complacent and contented person, and a droopy, languishing dog might very well indicate a weary and effete master.

What then can we say about the poodle, whose eagerness to please is not based upon ambition, whose gaiety is born in him? It is perfectly obvious that if you scratch the skin of a poodle owner you will find a hedonist—although a poodle never dares to be as pleasurable as he really is.

In buying a poodle puppy, bear in mind that you are bringing into your home a personality that demands regard and attention. He is an important adjunct to your life, a treasure that you are going to possess and cherish for many years. Profound thought should go into the matter of selection.

The best age at which to buy a dog is from three to five months, although many people buy at two months because they do not want to be deprived of the pleasure of watching the antics of a very young puppy. If, however, you are buying the animal with the idea of possibly exhibiting him, it is best to wait until he is six months old, and even then you cannot be too sure that he will be a perfect show specimen when he matures.

First you will have to consider size in making your choice. Do you want a standard, miniature, or toy? Your preference as to size, or variety, depends upon a number of factors of which you will have to be the sole judge. You may have an apartment which is so small that it precludes the presence of a standard, whereas, if you live in a country house, you may want a standard to protect the children and act as a watch dog. Generally speaking, the standard is a man's dog—strong, hardy, and rugged. The size of the miniature makes it an all-round type, able to adapt itself to any situation. One might almost say that the miniature variety could be considered feminine. Von Bensheim said that although the bark of the miniature contained a multitude of nuances, pyschologically the dog was feminine, and the *Cyclopedia of 1880* spoke of it as "much in request as a lady's pet."

The toy is just as true to type, as much of a poodle as the standard. It has the same conformation, bone structure, and general appearance (proportionately speaking) as the larger varieties. Considered by some as a bauble and by others as an ideal shopping companion, it nevertheless has traits and characteristics identical to those of its larger brothers. Its very diminutiveness, plus the scarcity of true types, greatly enhances its value.

Once you have decided on the variety, color must be considered. All in all you have six different colors and their variations from which to choose. Many English writers of a hundred years ago claimed that the blacks were superior in brain capacity, though Markham, as early as 1621, argued that color did not necessarily indicate superiority. At that time some claimed that blacks were the hardiest, browns the best swimmers, and particolors the best in scent. But, as Markham pointed out: "Yet in truth it is nothing so, for all colors are alike." And in 1803 a London writer profoundly wrote, when someone spoke of the superior intelligence of the blacks: "These are, however, more probably the prognostics of a fertile imagination than the judicious assertions of a well-founded observation."

The Germans developed the whites yet appeared to prefer to work with the browns on the stage or in the circus. The French for a long time back appeared partial to the blacks although they now seem to be favoring the browns. Some people will remember the charming pen-and-ink drawings of poodles by Caran d'Ache that became famous before the First World War and were reproduced, as the national dog of France, in jet and diamonds on cigarette cases and powder compacts. Anyway, attempts to rate the dog's intelligence in accordance with its color have no logical basis and have met with no general success, but certain it is that the blacks possess spark, spirit, and animation.

Mrs. David Greene of the Verdant Kennels, Connecticut, secretary of the Poodle Club of America for many years, is a breeder of browns and prefers their color for warmth, softness, and poodle expression. It is true of the browns that their eyes are not so dark as most breeders and judges prefer, but continued efforts are being made to remedy this. It is also true that the browns have a tendency to fade in the sun.

Lydia Hopkins of the Sherwood Hall Kennels, California, who has done considerable research work with brown poodles, has observed that a microscopic study of their hair shows that the granules are oval instead of round as in the other diluted colors of the granule pattern.

From this she infers that brown is the most recessive of the dilute colors. Should you favor the color, examine the pedigree of the puppy you buy, on both sides of the family, to make sure that there is a predominance of brown in the ancestry. The presence of black in the pedigree is not harmful but helpful. The browns include the various shades or dilutions such as cinnamon, café au lait, beaver, and the like.

The whites have majesty and dignity—a certain stateliness in the grand manner. Should you decide on buying a white, make sure that the eyes are very dark and the nose, lips, and eyelids solid black without any liver or lighter color spotting. Cream is a variation of the white, and the apricot and champagne colors are tender and desirable. There is also what is called a blue. This color is as difficult to describe as to find; it represents a dilution of black and is the color of dark smoke or slate. The gray is extremely popular in miniatures. It is somewhat of a rarity in toys. Few gray standards are available in the United States although breeding programs are now being carried on to insure this color a position. The true silver, or platinum, is exceedingly rare and expensive. It is usually found in miniatures and very occasionally in toys. It is uncommon in standards, and in the United States there are only a handful of specimens.

Bear in mind, too, in purchasing a gray or silver, that they are usually born black and the coat does not turn to its true color until the dog is nine or ten months old. It may take as long as eighteen months for the diluting factor to complete its effect. If at the end of eighteen months the coat is not of solid color the chances are it will never be so, and it will be impossible to exhibit your gray or silver as a poodle of solid color. If you are purchasing a puppy as gray or silver, examine the hair close to the skin of the feet, and if it shows a light gray or silver cast you can be reasonably sure the puppy will turn gray or silver. And, of course, you always have the benefit of the pedigree, which will give the color of the sire and dam and the breeder's word as to the color of puppies the dam has had when bred to the same sire.

Next comes the matter of sex. Although some people disagree, I am inclined to believe that dogs, like human beings, gravitate toward the opposite sex. Generally speaking, a male dog will attach himself to a woman, a female to a man, so if you are buying a puppy for your husband, and for him alone, consider buying a female. I hold it to be an unalterable truth that a man cannot possibly know anything about women until he has owned a girl poodle. If you are buying a puppy for your wife exclusively, then I suggest that you get a male. If you are buying a puppy for both husband and wife—well, you'll have to make up your own mind.

There are some people who find things a little difficult because of what a female poodle has to go through twice a year unless she is spayed, but it is probably no worse than having to stop at every lamp post and hydrant ten times a day. It is generally true that the female is more affectionate than the male, and rarely goes farther than the back door by herself. Happily, however, poodles of either sex are not wanderers.

You may prefer to eliminate all argument and purchase both a boy and a girl. As the author Josef Israels points out: "A French philosopher summed up the Gallic view of sex with *'Vive la différence!'* He was speaking, of course, about people, but the epigram goes for poodles as well. The poodle temperament shows, to a far greater extent than I have observed in any other breed, the difference in sex. In many strains of dogs the temperamental and personality difference between dog and bitch is considerably obscured by the predominant breed trait. In the cocker spaniel, for instance, the male is likely to be as tender and cuddly as the female. A lady Scotty will exhibit the same joyous or surly character as her male counterpart. But where poodles are concerned, the girl is very much the lady, and the gentleman is very much the boss of the family. You may not notice this so much unless you own a pair of poodles.

"My wife and I couldn't decide between a dog and a bitch, so we took both and have never regretted it. Wiener and Schnitzel complement each other and their owners completely. It has been little or no additional trouble to have the two of them, and the compensations have been more than ample. Schnitzel, the bitch, is thoroughly feminine and concentrates her wiles and attentions on male humans. A word of affection sends her into an ecstasy of tail-wagging, and at a kindly caress she rolls over for stomach scratching with the careless abandon of a trusting wanton. From the beginning she acknowledged the place of the larger and heavier Wiener as the head of the family. If there is a plaything, a bone, or even a tasty meal, Wiener has first rights. Schnitzel willingly surrenders her personal priorities to her lord and master, which he acknowledges gracefully but with little outward sign of affection.

"Only when another dog pays attention to Schnitzel does Wiener raise his hackles, growl protectingly, and slip as lightly as a mongoose between his mate and the male interloper. He has a steady independence, a respectability, and an entirely masculine outlook on lady dogs. If they see fit to recognize his superiority—well, that's the least that's due him. Only once, when Schnitzel was feeling super-possessive about her first litter of pups, did Wiener take orders from her. She told him firmly that he wasn't to put so much as an inquisitive paw or nostril inside the puppy box, and when he tried it she slapped him down. In recognition of this maternal achievement Wiener even surrendered first rights at the supper dish until the puppies were old enough to compete, and then he showed them, too, who was boss.

"If there is a moral in this for prospective poodle owners, it is that I hope they will get a pair as I did, but if you intend to acquire only one, try to investigate some fair samples of male and female poodles before making your choice. Personally I don't go along with those who would make a firm rule of a bitch for a man and a dog for a woman, although such choices usually work out well. As in art, music, or the selection of the right wine to complement your meal, it is not so much what you ought to have but what you like that counts. Me, I like boy and girl poodles—together!"

When you have your mind fairly well made up as to what you really want, go to an established and recognized breeder specializing in that variety, or speak to a qualified representative of kennels and make known your desires. Depending upon time and distance, the breeder may bring the puppy to you for examination, or you may have to travel to the kennels. It is considered inadvisable to purchase a puppy at a pet shop maintained for both boarding and selling dogs; from the very nature of things, sanitary conditions are not of the best, and the possibility of sickness is too great a risk. In addition, the presence of poodle puppies on such premises frequently means distress merchandise. So if you are the sort of person who loves dogs, and things like spring in the air, the scent of newly turned earth, and the first frost slithering the hedgerows on a hunting morning, don't go into a pet shop. If you do your heart will probably melt at the sight of a beseeching animal begging for attention. You'll be haunted by a pair of pleading black eyes and a small wet nose pressed against the bars of a cage, and you'll either be overpowered by an irresistible impulse then and there, or you will go back and buy him the next day.

Occasionally individuals who are not established breeders have a litter, find that they cannot raise the puppies, and so are forced to put them out for sale. Often enough these puppies are of excellent blood lines and have been well brought up. But in such instances be sure, before looking at them, that you examine the pedigree and that the litter is registered. Find out the name of the breeder, and if there is any doubt in your mind, get in touch with him.

Contrary to the popular belief, the poodle breeder does not make money in the raising and selling of puppies. Breeders are primarily fanciers, interested in popularizing the breed and introducing it into new fields of endeavor. They are constantly working with new and old blood lines, trying to develop and perfect the most desirable qualities. They are forever attempting, by scientific breeding, to lower the ear, improve the shape of the face, achieve more darkness in the eyes, a better skull, legs, muzzle, and so on. This is all to your advantage, and it must be realized that nature is slow and that only by just degrees does it achieve perfection.

Mrs. L. W. Bonney of the Tally-Ho Kennels, Oyster Bay, New York, points out: "It has often been said that it costs no more to feed a good dog than a poor one, so whether a buyer wants a poodle for exhibition, breeding, or companionship, there is but one place to purchase a dog, and that is from an established kennel whose stock is registered with the American Kennel Club. Usually the best pedigree is the name of the breeder. The fact that the stock is so registered is a guarantee to the purchaser that the puppy he buys is a hundred per cent poodle—that is, purebred. Many breeders advertise in various canine magazines that if one is uncertain about a breeder in a specific territory, the American Kennel Club will furnish all necessary information. In addition to being convinced about the breeding of a dog purchased from such a reliable source, you will be dealing with someone who wants you to be satisfied, who wants the puppy to be satisfied, and who will be of every possible assistance in advising you how best to train, raise, and care for your pet."

You may be anxious to buy a good puppy, but conscientious breeders are also worried about the dog having a good home. Don't feel unduly offended if they inquire into your private life and surroundings. You must satisfy them that you have more to offer the puppy than the puppy has to offer you. It is not what you have that counts—it is what you are. Most dogs, and particularly poodles, can adjust themselves to almost any situation within reason. They are possessive creatures and make their decisions about the people they like with an uncanny insight. They are proud, too, in the placing of their affections, and just a wee bit snobbish. No matter how kind and thoughtful may be the kennel man, cook, or chauffeur who feeds and walks him, the dog will turn tail and drop them like a cold waffle at the sound of his master's voice. Of course I don't mean that this sort of thing should be carried too far, like the Russian countess whose aristocratic and neurotic Borzoi would shake like an arrowroot blanc-mange every time the new footman brought him his platter because he simply couldn't abide the color of his hair. There is nothing more annoying than a spoiled and pampered animal, and nobody should "give his heart to a dog to tear," as Kipling said, although many of us do so unconsciously.

But love, common sense, and regular personal care are indispensable to the life span and happiness of your poodle. Poodles have an ingrained sense of decency and are precise in the way they do things; they know when it is right time for bed, feeding, exercise. They like cleanliness in their bedding and grooming, and this quality is especially marked in bitches. The naive vanity of the poodle is a heritage from generations of grooming, brushing, and clipping, handed down, perhaps, from those kingly dogs, the famous *chiens d'eau* of Louis the Fourteenth of France, who roamed the green velvet parterres of Versailles with beribboned topknots and collars of silver bells.

A distinct advantage in buying from an established breeder is that many of them will take the puppy back after four or five days if you don't feel satisfied. This is not so much because you are displeased, but because they do not want their puppy to be with a discontented person. The animal will be sold to you in a healthy, sound condition. Some breeders insist on having it examined by a veterinarian just before the sale, and on furnishing you with a certificate of good health. If you feel there is anything wrong with your purchase, by all means request that it be examined before you take it.

Human association being more important to the poodle than anything else, you should assure yourself that the puppy has had plenty of human companionship since being whelped. Puppies born and brought up in kennels, far away from the house and the sound of human voices, may have a tendency to be stand-offish and shy. I have an idea that all kennels so situated should have a radio installed so that the puppies can become accustomed to hearing different human voices. Many breeders, when their puppies are a month or so old, devote an hour a day to playing with them in the house, one by one, in order to determine their traits and personalities.

Robert S. Emerson of the Star Tavern Kennels, Pipersville, Pennsylvania, raises his puppies to be fearless and aggressive. After selling them, he has often had the opportunity to observe their later progress in the hands of their new owners. He had found that some became timid. Inquiring into the reason for the change, he ascertained that it was because the owner had either boarded the puppy out for a period of time or had in some other way deprived it of human companionship.

The matter of a shy puppy always brings up the subject of heredity versus environment, that is, which is the more important. Mrs. E. A. Stein of the Samarkand Kennels, Port Washington, New York, says: "I have very definite convictions on the subject of heredity versus environment. I feel that how a poodle puppy is brought up is what counts. How much love and affection is lavished upon him, how he is taught to behave—those are the important factors in shaping his disposition. I base my feelings on more breeds than just poodles, as I have bred, raised, and owned dogs of several other varieties which are supposedly 'one-man' dogs, German shepherds, schnauzers and Sealyhams—and I have never raised a shy or mean dog."

It is submitted that, with respect to poodles, environment is a more important factor than heredity. To paraphrase an old Spanish proverb, "It is not necessary to inquire too closely into a good poodle's ancestry"—not necessary because the blood lines, or the inherited traits and characteristics, are well known and firmly guarded by poodle breeders who are ever on the alert against the infusion of undesirable or unproved blood into their strain. Practically all of the desirable sires are available only to approved bitches, which means that the owner of the sire has the right to decide, after studying the bitch's pedigree, whether a mating would spell out an unhappy result. It is true that lately there have been a few individuals who, without the necessary knowledge and experience in such matters, have been breeding poodles as an avocation, impulsively risking nothing but gaining nothing. Fortunately such amateur breeders sooner or later run into the law of diminishing returns, with the result that their particular strain is not perpetuated.

So, if the poodle has the blood and the goodly heritage, it is necessary only to add proper upbringing in a fitting environment.

If a puppy is shy at the age of six months or over, pass it up. The saying "You gets what you pay for" is a true one. There are no bargains in poodles. The more money you pay, the better the dog. People constantly ask me where they can find an exceedingly fine specimen and explain that they do not want the dog for show purposes but only for a companion. I have pointed out to them the similarity of buying a mink coat. After all, you pay for value, and the furrier doesn't care a hoot whether you want the coat to wear to a horse show or to the corner delicatessen.

Before attempting to buy a puppy, study the points of the ideal poodle closely.[1] When you examine the puppy, see that the forelegs come straight from the shoulders. Look for dark eyes, with emphasis on their oval shape, and see that the eyes are sufficiently wide apart to indicate ample brain capacity. A dark brown cast in the eyes of a black, evidencing brown in the ancestry, is not objectionable; indeed, in the opinion of many experts, it adds to the earnestness of expression. Be very sure that the dew-claws are off. See that the ears are set low and hang close to the head. Look at the tail, which, to me, is the hallmark of the poodle. Be sure that it is set on fairly high, of proper length (about five vertebrae), and carried merrily with all the insouciance of a gay blade.

The price for standards does not vary in accordance with color. Nor does it vary with miniatures, except that silver will be more costly. As miniatures are more expensive than standards, so are toys more expensive than miniatures. This is because, with all due respect to the toy, good brood bitches are rare, and the number of puppies whelped is few. Toys are to be found mostly in white or cream, sometimes gray, and some good blacks are being developed now.

Remember, however, this rule: a poodle should be of a solid color, whatever it is. Do not buy a mismarked or particolored animal; it cannot be exhibited, and you will find it difficult to breed since the chances are that the puppies will also be mismarked. In an established kennel you can rest assured that you will not be shown such an animal. The ability to produce mismarkeds and particolors is inherited, and breeders take the utmost precautions to prevent their procreation. Mismarking, by the way, generally consists of white or contrasting patches in the coat; it occurs principally on the chest, belly, and feet.

Don't be too reticent in explaining just what type of puppy you are looking for. The puppies in a litter may seem alike but they are not. They have been watched since whelping, and the breeder knows all about their little tricks and quirks. He will tell you, "This boy is a regular Humphrey Bogart"; or, "This little girl is demure, and a natural charmer." You may not see the best puppy in the litter, for the breeder might want to keep it for possible show purposes. (Even if you did see it you probably wouldn't pay the price asked.) Nevertheless,

[1] See page 125 for description of the ideal poodle by the Poodle Club of America.

study the puppies you are offered carefully, and observe the habits and characteristics of each. In a short time one of them will reach out in some mystical fashion, and "Zing . . ." will go the strings of your heart. The wind-up will be that you have the puppy you want, and the puppy will know it.

No one ever actually sold a puppy. A puppy sells itself, it talks to you with "speaking eyes." There is something occult about the procedure. I recall what happened to me a few years ago when I bought a puppy, a son of Ch. Eiger, from Mrs. Sherman R. Hoyt, Blakeen Kennels, Stamford, Connecticut. The four-months-old apricot litter was playing about in an outdoor enclosure, and as I approached all of them ran toward me and clawed the tall wire fence like mad, begging me to take them home—that is, all except one.

In the center of the pen was a large telephone pole, and one of the puppies remained behind it but repeatedly showed me half of his face. I watched him carefully from across the fifteen feet that separated us—he was winking at me! I simply couldn't believe it. Then, a second later, the other half of his face appeared on the opposite side of the pole. He could wink with both eyes. He was telling me, "Don't pay any attention to those eager beavers. I am the jester who wants to take over your court"—and he did. I have never seen such an ambidextral poodle since.

Another advantage in seeing the litter is the opportunity afforded of looking over the dam. Ancestors are to be reckoned with, and you might bear in mind the practice of experienced suitors: see the girl-friend's mama—c'est la même chose? You should diligently inspect the dam and study her for points and mannerisms you may like or dislike.

Make certain that the puppy is registered or registerable, though this will always be so in an established kennel. When a whelping occurs, the breeder registers the entire litter with the American Kennel Club, and you should receive from the breeder a form entitled "Application for Registration of Dog of Registered Litter." This application must be signed by the breeder and must record the litter number and other details. Just send it in to the American Kennel Club and have the dog registered in your name.

It may be that the puppy is individually registered. In that case, the breeder will sign the certificate of registration and transfer it to you so that you can send it in and procure a certificate of registration number in your own name. You should also secure a signed pedigree, which most breeders will furnish unasked. Always insist that the pedigree show the color of each of the pup's ancestors for three generations back. You will require this information should you decide to breed in the future.

The breeder may or may not clip the puppy in the style you desire and you can of course have this attended to later.

Taking the pup home, you should provide some precautions against car-sickness. Carry along a large towel—if you are a novice you might as well get used to this sort of thing at once—and if the puppy is not fed for a couple of hours or so before he undertakes his journey, and if the bowels have moved in the meantime, the chances of car-sickness will be minimized. Car-sickness is a form of nervousness, and there is practically no cure for it except to continue to take the animal out driving until the condition is cured. Should the puppy have to be shipped by air, freight, or train, have no fears. Regardless of the length of the trip he will greet you with a joyous wagging of his tail when he arrives.

In picking up the puppy, or any puppy for that matter, do not grasp him under the forelegs and jerk, for a sad case of hernia may result, and puppies are most susceptible to this type of injury. Get down and give support to the stern. Place the right hand under the hindquarters, the left hand under the right foreleg by the shoulder, and lift gently. The transformation of the puppy, from a toughie on the floor to a piece of soft melted butter in your arms, will be instantaneous.

Another dangerous habit indulged in by both novices and the experienced is that of grabbing a puppy by the loose skin of the neck and shoulders. If a puppy or dog is lifted in this manner, a straining of the axillary glands might result, and in some cases discomfort and pain. Repeated liftings of this sort will surely result in malformation of the shoulders of a growing dog.

The breeder should furnish you with the diet the puppy has been used to, and this should be strictly followed for a few days. After a while you can modify it in accordance with your own household requirements, but such changes ought to be made only after you have experimented and observed the effects.

The breeder will also tell you what has already been done by way of immunization against distemper. Practically all breeders take these precautionary measures, but it is agreed that puppies under five and six months of age cannot receive complete immunity from inoculations, since preliminary shots at this age are not one hundred per cent effective. Still, every puppy should have them with the hope that they may be effective in his particular case. Incidentally, if the teeth of your puppy show, after teething, a series of small brown spots that look like stains, be grateful. This means that the puppy has had a slight attack of distemper undetected by the breeder, and that he undoubtedly has complete immunity.

Also, find out if the puppy has been wormed and make a note of the date on the pedigree. He will probably require further worming in two or three months.

The armful of happiness is about to enter your home. Are you prepared to render to him the things that are his, adorn him with a good disposition, and mold his life with such purpose and thought that you will be able to proclaim, as did Alexander Woollcott of his poodle: "No creature on earth I find more entertaining, and none in the warmth of whose generous heart I place more implicit trust"?

chapter 3

FEEDING AND NUTRITION

Sit down and feed, and welcome to our table.
AS YOU LIKE IT

GOLDSMITH POINTED OUT THAT THE DOG IS THE ONLY animal who, "leaving his fellows, attempts to cultivate the friendship of man." Although this union in friendly living occurred several thousand years ago, there still is a considerable amount of controversy on what a dog should eat. The dog, on the other hand, views such argument as utter nonsense and gives himself trustingly and completely over to your protection. He knows that his proper diet is just what you yourself eat, and that if there is one thing man should have learned through his centuries of association with the dog it is that the laws of nutrition are remarkably alike for both. Indeed, there are only a few differences, such as the advisability of eliminating sugar and foods excessive in starch content from the diet, but a dog's stomach can digest even these.

All this may sound reassuringly simple. At the same time, a great many canine gastric disturbances and diseases may be caused by faulty feeding, so it cannot be overemphasized that nutrition, having a great deal to do with substance, is the most important factor in a dog's existence. Remember that the function of correct alimentation is to insure for your pet a long life and a healthy one, and that good food such as you eat yourself is more than just an intake of nourishment; digestion, absorption, metabolism, and elimination are also involved. With a poodle the correct functioning of these things means bright eyes, a gay tail, a sturdy coat free from skin ailment, and an all-round alertness and vivacity.

I have never been able to understand how some people—really nice people—so frequently grow careless about the welfare of their pets. Once the novelty of having them has worn off a bit, they may leave their dog's feeding to a temperamental cook or harassed maid. They don't realize, perhaps, that a mess of soggy biscuits or hunks of greasy meat are as distasteful and depressing to a hungry dog as a staple diet of tepid porridge would be to human beings. They do not stop to read the appeal in their dog's eyes, or notice the pathetic droop of his tail as he turns disappointedly away after the first mouthful of some nauseating concoction. They say, "Oh, he'll eat it all right when he gets good and hungry!" There is no more selfish and ignorant phrase. Refined dogs, especially poodles and the smaller varieties, will not eat any old thing when they are hungry. They won't eat what they don't like—and that's that!

But let us go back to the advent of a poodle puppy in this work-a-day world and trace his alimentary progress. Actually, his nutrition began before he was whelped, and depended on the manner in which his dam was fed and cared for before being bred and while carrying her litter. You have had no control over that, of course, but deficiencies are bound to occur now and then, even with the most careful breeder, and it is up to you to give your puppy the best of nourishment.

Puppies are usually weaned when they are six weeks old. During the nursing period they live almost entirely on their mother's milk, and this milk contains all the nutrition they require except possibly Vitamins A and E. The competent breeder will, before weaning, gradually accustom the puppies to solid bits of food so that no dislocation will occur after they are weaned. At about four weeks he will hand-feed them finely shredded, raw, or slightly seared meat, and a wheat cereal in evaporated milk to which a little lime water has been added. For toys and very small puppies, fresh round steak scraped with a knife to a jelly-like substance and moistened with a few drops of warm water is excellent.

After weaning, the important thing is to transfer the puppies to a solid diet as soon as possible, with food that will provide the essentials for bone and body building. At two months of age a puppy should eat five or six meals a day; from three to six months, at least three meals a day; from six months to a year, twice daily; and at a year one well-rounded meal once a day.

The main feed for a puppy should consist of meat, eggs, milk, and cereals. Nutrition-wise, it is not entirely necessary for a young puppy to have vegetables until he is about eight or nine months old, when they may be added to the diet and the amount gradually increased. However, it is recommended that a small amount of vegetables, preferably in baby food form, be mixed in the puppy's main meal so that he will become accustomed to them and will not consider them repugnant when his system requires them.

Meat represents the major portion of a dog's meal. It may be beef, horse meat, lamb, mutton, or the glandular organs such as beef liver, beef kidney, beef or veal heart, spleen, and tripe, the latter well cooked. Pork is usually considered taboo because of the possible presence of trichinosis, but it ranks high in nutritive value, and boiled pig liver is considered excellent for puppies. When we talk about meat we are, of course, talkng about protein, the builder of muscles and organs. Protein is also present in soy bean meal, dried skim milk, brewer's yeast, cream and cottage cheese, fish, peanut butter, and, in limited amounts, in vegetables. Protein is an organic compound utilized almost completely by the dog. When protein is taken into the body it breaks down into amino acids, and these acids enter the blood stream and build and rebuild the tissue. All protcin contains not less than twenty-three amino acids, and of these twenty-three at least ten are required by the dog. These ten are arginine, histidine, isoleucine, leucine, lysine, methionine, phenylalanine, threonine, tryptophane, and valine. It is absolutely essential that all of these be present in the protein of the food. If a single one of them is not present, an impairment of the health or some organic deficiency will result.

Meat may be fed raw or cooked, depending on the taste of the dog. Some serve raw meat one day and cooked the next. Raw meat contains slightly more moisture than cooked. Although many experts feel that cooking meat is a waste of time and tends to destroy vitamin content, there is ample authority for saying that slightly cooked meat is more easily digestible and more nutritious than raw. Obviously meat should never be fried, as this does destroy certain nutritive elements. The cheaper cuts of lean meat are preferable as they possess more vitamin content. Chuck and muscle meat are superior to sirloin. Muscle meat is so rich in protein that if a dog were fed this alone he would soon die of constipation, for the meat would be one hundred per cent digestible. Muscle meat has a generous supply of Vitamin B, and kidneys contain desirable minerals such as iron. Liver is rich in Vitamin A and especially recommended for puppies, although not in quantity since the iron in it tends to consume the fat-soluble vitamins. Lamb contains an abundance of fat and may be fed frequently when a building-up process is necessary, but, like liver, should be given sparingly to puppies. Skin and the tendons of fowl are not digestible. Fish, which should be provided occasionally, say, once a week, contains less protein than meat; therefore more fish by volume should be given. Salmon and tuna are the best, but make sure that the fish is completely boned.

Vegetables commonly used are carrots, spinach, onions, beets, tomatoes, string beans, peas. You may be derided by some people for feeding your dog vegetables. You will be told, "Meat is the only diet for a dog—vegetables do no good." The speaker may pretend to know a great deal about dogs, but actually he knows very little about nutrition. As Faust said in his soliloquy in the presence of the black poodle, "Men are accustomed to deride what they do not understand."

All authorities on dog nutrition agree that vegetables are essential for their mineral and vitamin content, plus their efficacy as a bowel mover. Dandelion greens, spinach, and beet greens provide Vitamin A. Onions, broccoli, kale, and collards furnish calcium and phosphorus. Carrots and beets should be boiled to release their starch content and served mashed or ground. Many dogs, however, eat carrots in the raw state and cannot get enough. Of all vegetables, carrots are probably the best for Vitamin A content. Wash and scrape a carrot and let your dog chew it like a bone, or shred it into his meal. Tomatoes are especially good and may also be fed raw or cooked, according to the dog's preference. Tomato pomace is a miracle item and has a salutary effect in the curing of diarrhea. String beans are hard to digest and not particularly recommended, although I know of dogs that thrive on them. Peas are gas-forming and undesirable from a standpoint of digestibility. Cooked onions are always a treat. As for potatoes, all of us seem to have a phobia against feeding them to a dog, yet experiments have indicated that dogs fed on potatoes alone for a considerable length of time received sufficient nourishment and no deficiencies resulted. So, contrary to popular belief, a dog can make use of cooked starch.

In the field of cereals there are various dried foods on the market. They come in four types: meal, biscuits, pellets, and kibbled—that is, broken up into small chunks. These foods contain wheat and oat flours, alfalfa meal, soy bean oil, fried skim milk, corn middlings. The kibbled variety is preferred because dogs like chunky food. These dried foods are low in fat content, otherwise they would soon become rancid. They have to be moistened with hot water, vegetable water, or poultry broth.

Fat is essential to dogs. It performs the same function as it does for human beings: gives insulation and builds up a food reserve. Excess body fat, though, is to be avoided, as it makes for an inactive, slovenly dog. A dog's meal should contain not less than seven per cent fat, and some hold that it is perfectly permissible that twenty-five per cent of the meal consist of fat. The fat in meat varies in accordance with the cut. The ordinary cuts contain about eight per cent fat, which is sufficient for all purposes. To supplement this you may frequently feed the well-cooked tail of a steak or lamb chop.

It is often said that dogs who receive a properly balanced and nutritious diet do not require vitamins. This is partly true, but it does not tell the whole story. We have all seen people who eat properly but become afflicted with some ailment arising from vitamin deficiency; the vitamins were taken into the system but the system did not absorb them. It is precisely the same with dogs. Puppies are weaned with a certain deficiency of Vitamins A and E, which are fat-soluble vitamins. Vitamin A has already been mentioned in connection with the foods in which it is found.

Fish liver oils such as cod liver oil and the halibut oils provide Vitamin D as well as A. Puppies should be fed these oils mixed in with their food. Be careful about giving overdoses as sickness may result. In the summer time, if the animal is getting plenty of sunshine, it may not be necessary to supply oil, but if you find it advisable, see that it is kept in a cool place.

Vitamin E, originally known as the reproductive or fertility vitamin, is the wonder vitamin so far as poodle breeders are concerned, and I cannot help feeling that they were the first to discover its magic qualities, its remarkable effect on the dog's skin and coat. Lately there has been some reason to believe that it also makes for better eyesight and muscle support. In its ordinary form Vitamin E is packaged as a wheat-germ oil. It should be given to puppies as soon as they are weaned and continued for life at a teaspoonful a day. Unlike fish oil, it does not become rancid.

Steamed bone meal is the best natural source of calcium and phosphorus and should be mixed with the puppy's main meal, if the dog doesn't go for cod liver oil. About one per cent of the meal should be supplied by this mineral. Dried brewer's yeast furnishes Vitamin B₁, and iron is found in liver, kidneys, and egg yolks. By the way, don't think that your dog has gone feminine if he suddenly devours a fruit salad. The Vitamin A in the leaves of vegetables is utilized by the dog and the same vitamin, together with iron, is found in prunes, peaches, and apricots.

Your dog's food dish should be of the correct type and size. Secure a bowl designed so that the ears cannot fall into it. If food particles remain on the tips of the ears they will attract vermin. The bowl should have a concave bottom, which is not only better for eating but makes cleaning easier. It should be reasonably heavy, too, so it cannot be pushed around. Most dogs do not relish vegetables and cereals too keenly, consequently all foods of this kind, including Vitamin E, should be thoroughly mixed and blended together before going into the bowl.

As the teeth of the dog are designed for tearing and not chewing, it is only natural for him to gulp his food. Dogs like to be given their food in chunks, bolt it, and then the stomach takes over.

Every week or so, cut up finely a clove of garlic and mix well with the feed. The garlic will counteract any excessive intestinal acidity.

For a tidbit after dinner, give your poodle a ginger snap. It is alleged that the saliva in a dog's mouth does not contain ptyalin, the enzyme found in the saliva of human beings that acts as the first agent to convert starches into body sugar. The ginger snap, however, will induce the flow of saliva in the dog's mouth, which is bound to have some beneficial action in the digestive process.

Of course, there is no purebred aristocratic canine who won't have a go at the garbage can now and again and snitch some tempting and malodorous morsel with the greatest relish. Morbid appetite, you say? Not at all. Dogs will be dogs, and, after all, probably such a decadent taste is no worse than the human gourmet who gorges himself on a really high breast of pheasant or a moldering and fruity concoction of Bombay Duck. Needless to say, the garbage-can complex must be firmly discouraged, as must the picking up of any stray scraps outdoors, particularly in cities where poisoned meat is often left on the street and in parks to kill rats, or by some vicious crackpot who hates animals. It is an excellent idea to teach your dog to refuse anything whatsoever offered by strangers, and to train him to be as much as possible a one-man dog.

A dog asks so little and gives so much that again I say: make it a duty to set aside a little time from your personal problems to look after his meals yourself whenever possible. Believe me, it will pay divi-

photos by Ylla

Wiener and Schnitzel and their two puppies,
owned by Josef Israels II

photo by Lineer

Sherwood Petite Paillette. By Ch. Sherwood Pocket Edition—Sherwood Charmeuse. Black toy owned by Sherwood Hall Kennels, Redwood City, California. It took Lydia Hopkins years of study and selective breeding to perfect this true-to-type toy.

Ch. Robinhood. By Sunstorm's Snuff—Cartlane Marguerite. Brown standard owned by Helvan Kennels, Norfolk, Massachusetts. Winner of Best in Show at the Poodle Club of America Specialty Show at Garden City, New York, May 19, 1950.

photo by Evelyn M. Shafer

Ch. Tilo Blase, C. D. By Bibelot Cadet of Misty Isles—Ch. Far Away Katy Did, U. D. Gray miniature owned by Tilo Kennels, Bay Shore, New York.

photo by Tauskey

An unposed photograph of Jester. Spying a rabbit about a hundred yards away, Jester bounded onto a nearby table and assumed this faultless position pointing the rabbit.

Ch. Carillon Jester, U. D. T., Int. C. D. By Ch. White Cockade of Salmagundi—Ch. Carillon Colline.

One of America's top-ranking obedience-trained dogs, Jester is known the world over through his exhibitions in films and in the field. Owned by Carillon Kennels, Pawling, New York.

photo by Tauskey

Ch. Cartlane Once. By Ch. Leicester's Bonbon—Cartlane Odette. This white toy, owned by Mrs. Charles R. Fleishman, North Hollywood, California, has run up a sensational record in the ring. Shown thirty-eight times, she has won Best of Variety thirty-six times. She has twenty-three firsts in the toy group and thirteen seconds. She has gone Best American-Bred in Show five times, was named the best bitch poodle, all sizes, at the Poodle Club of America Specialty Show at Garden City, New York, on May 19, 1950. She has gone Best in Show three times. She has never been defeated since graduating from the puppy classes.

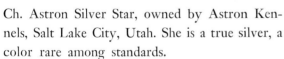

Ch. Astron Silver Star, owned by Astron Kennels, Salt Lake City, Utah. She is a true silver, a color rare among standards.

photo by Chandler

photos by Tauskey

Ch. Ensarr Glacé. By Ch. Lucite of Salmagundi—Ch. Pillicoc Pearl. Owned by Ensarr Kennels, Bernardsville, New Jersey. Shown in puppy clip at nine months.

Ch. Ensarr Glacé in show clip at maturity

Leicester's Sunlight on Snow. By Ch. Leicester's Peaches and Cream—Lafferty's Ma Chère. White toy owned by Mrs. H. S. Yung of New York and Hong Kong.

photo by Evelyn M. Shafer

Ch. Belle Isle Bright Gem. By Ch. Hollycourt Manicamp—Cartlane Petite Platina.
Silver miniature owned by Strathglass Kennels, Port Chester, New York

Miss Matilda, white toy owned by Mrs. James Lowell Oakes, Jr.

White toys owned by Mrs. James M. Austin, Catawba Kennels,
Old Westbury, New York

dends. Think up little changes and pleasures for his diet; no single regime can provide all the necessary minerals and vitamins he needs. Besides, your veterinarian will tell you that many kinds of skin diseases and stomach disorders can arise from lack of them.

Some puppies, especially while teething, and some grown dogs, go off-feed for a few days or even longer. This, even when it recurs, should cause no mental anguish, as it is merely nature's way. There is nothing you can do about it. But if it isn't one thing it's another. Ilka Chase, a poodle pantologist if there ever was one, frequently becomes exasperated with her miniature, Mr. Puffle, and says despairingly, "He is a distraction because of his appetite. I look with envy at the ads for dog food showing happy canines either rushing madly to their bowls of Pard, Dash, Gaines, or Dog Yummy's, tongues awash, or sitting, eyes bright, ears pricked, beside the polished dish. My poodle is not like that. His preference is for humming birds' tongues done with garlic and a dry white wine, or the white meat of frogs' legs. Not only does it take a good deal of time to find humming birds' tongues but a vast deal of work to be able to afford them, yet I do my feeble best.

"Oh, we have had endurance tests to see who could hold out the longer. I have placed tasty horse meat and uncompromising biscuits in front of him, saying sternly, 'Either you eat this or you go without.' He has gone as long as three days without. Something had to snap. It was me. He now eats what he likes."

The important points to remember are: (1) Feed regularly; (2) Feed balanced meals; (3) Feed a varied diet.

A DO and DON'T guide for feeding may be summarized as follows:

DO Feed on a regular schedule, at the same time and place daily, with nothing to eat in between except a dog biscuit for the teeth. (Charcoal ones are good occasionally.)

DO Get your dog accustomed to all kinds of food while a puppy so that he will not become finicky later in life.

DO Make certain the food dish is clean before feeding. Always scald after feeding.

DO Feed a balanced diet; i.e., sixty per cent meat, twenty per cent cereal, and twenty per cent vegetables (for mature dogs).

DO Give the dog exercise after his main meal.

DO Have plenty of fresh, cool, and clean drinking water available at all times.

DO Supplement diet by giving vitamins if necessary.

DON'T Feed ice-cold or hot food.

DON'T Feed sloppy food. Dogs relish chunky, chewy foods.

DON'T Give any bones except knuckle or marrow.

The object in feeding a puppy is that he shall acquire weight and substance, and grow rapidly. Though a puppy two months of age should be fed five times a day, he should not be overstuffed. It is the frequency that is important.

BREAKFAST One-half cup of milk, room temperature. Mix with pablum to even consistency. Mix in a small amount of melted butter.

LUNCH Three tablespoons of ground meat either raw or slightly boiled.

AFTERNOON TEA One-half cup of meat or chicken broth with piece of whole-wheat toast.

DINNER Three tablespoons of ground meat to which has been added a teaspoonful of cod liver oil and a teaspoonful of wheat-germ oil.

BEFORE RETIRING A small quantity of milk.

The above menu and those following are for standards. For a miniature reduce by forty per cent, and for a toy reduce by eighty per cent.

When the puppy reaches three months of age there should be an increase in the amount of food and the meals may be cut down to three a day.

BREAKFAST Pour milk over one cup of crumbled shredded wheat. A small amount of melted butter may be added, and every other day a well-beaten egg yolk mixed in with the milk. Cooked cereals may be given instead, such as Cream of Wheat, oatmeal (not rolled oats), Wheatena, or farina.

LUNCH About one cup of ground meat either raw or slightly cooked. Mix in a teaspoonful of Karo syrup.

DINNER One cup of ground meat, raw or slightly cooked, to which add two teaspoonsful of mashed carrots, one teaspoonful of cod liver oil, and one teaspoonful of wheat-germ oil. Mix together and serve.

NIGHT A puppy biscuit.

Between the ages of six months and one year the puppy should have at least two meals a day with a constant increase in volume. Milk is part of his diet at this age only as a moistening agent. The puppy will have completed his teething by this time and will begin to relish chunky food.

BREAKFAST   About two cups of milk mixed with the dry or cooked cereal he thrives best on. Every other day mix in the well-beaten yolk of an egg. One slice of whole-wheat toast, buttered.

DINNER   Two cups of meat, one-half cup of vegetables, and one-half cup of cereal in kibbled form. Add one-half teaspoon of steamed bone meal, one teaspoon of wheat-germ oil, and mix together.

When the puppy is one year old he may be limited to one meal a day, this meal to be served either at noontime or in the evening, depending upon the most convenient time for him to be exercised. This should not be construed as a prohibition against his having a little toast and coffee with you in the morning. He, too, may want to start the day off with a bang!

Regularity of feeding is essential; it will prevent a dog from going off-feed and assure him of getting food that has not been spoiled by exposure. The poodle is a veritable time clock and will insist on being served at the same hour religiously. To him, feeding is a rite, a ceremony, and a pleasure that he has looked forward to all day.

Don't forget that the diet balance of sixty per cent meat, twenty per cent cereal, and twenty per cent vegetables is for mature dogs. This balance may be modified in accordance with habits. For example, if your dog is outdoors a great deal and indulging in more than the usual amount of exercise, he will require more energy-giving food—that is, meat. But if he lounges around an apartment all day he will need less of it.

Cool, fresh water is as indispensable to him as it is to you. The container, like the feeding bowl, should always be clean; in fact, scalded daily. The poodle is a fastidious feeder who likes to eat out of utensils that are scrupulously kept. I have often been asked about ice water, and can only reply that this is a matter of preference: some people like ice in their drinks, others do not, and dogs are the same. However, in the heat of the summer "dog days" I can see no objection to cooling the drinking water with ice. If a dog licks an ice cube, the water will be body temperature anyway before it reaches the stomach, although if he chews and swallows it rapidly the ice might cause an intestinal disturbance. Eating snow, by the way, is not bad in small quantities as it provides moisture, but too much is not good.

Many poodles have a habit of eating grass. Mine does. With most dogs this indicates a nauseous condition and assists in the throwing up of bile. Not with mine, and not with Alex, the standard owned by Norman Norell, New York's famous dress designer. Alex is partial to grass but eats only a specific type—no other. Norell had the type examined by a botanist, had to drive to Massachusetts to buy the seed, and planted it in the flowerboxes on his terrace.

There are on the market, by the way, many commercially prepared canned dog foods consisting of cooked meat by-products, cereals and cereal products, vegetables and vegetable products, ground bone and mineral matter. These are known as "wet foods." It is essential to read the labels carefully to determine whether the food contains at least the minimum percentage of the nutrients required by your dog. Most of these foods are characterized by a moisture content of about seventy-five per cent, which is not economical. Such canned foods are also known as "normal maintenance" food. Any product labeled "Complete Ration" should have the seal of the American Veterinary Medical and Animal Hospital Association.

The poodles of the circus are the most interesting examples of proper conditioning. They are usually fed to weight, like show dogs, and the amounts adjusted to how much exercise they get in the rings and in their training. Most performing dogs have extraordinarily retentive memories, especially poodles, whose sense of routine and timing is phenomenal. Of all the breeds they enjoy their work the most. Their natural vanity is gratified by it, they learn easily, and their keen intelligence prevents the tricks they do from growing burdensome or nerve-racking. Every circus trainer knows what each animal he is breaking in can do best, basing his judgment on body formation, muscular energy, so forth. He finds out in the early stages of training some particular ability in the dog and turns it to advantage. The lightness and supple strength of the poodle make him ideal for speed and jumping feats. Far back in circus history, from the time of the famous white toys or "dancing dogs" that were brought to England in 1700, poodles of all sizes have been show dogs par excellence. Their resilience, energy, adaptability, and intelligence are the main reasons for this, but their hardy system when properly fed, their superb bone structure and sound bodies, have been found to surpass all other breeds in the circus ring.

Most troupes of performing dogs have their traveling boxes either in trailers or trains and during long jumps must be exercised at least twice a day. Even so, traveling is hard on them and cuts down on fresh air and exercise, except when they are on open-air show lots. Their feeding problems are therefore crucial. Naturally, since they provide a livelihood for their owners, illness or loss of a star canine is a serious matter. Canned meat is used largely for convenience, but some trainers carry air-tight glass jars in which they simmer the best quality of meat and vegetables in a little water over a low flame to conserve the greatest values in juices and nourishment. Each dog is fed separately and to weight, generally after the last performance, and then exercised.

In the circus ring the reward of a malted-milk tablet for a successful trick brings surprising results. The wise trainer carries a few in his pocket during the act, and so do many show handlers, although some use bits of liver. There is no greater treat for a dog than this simple nourishing tidbit, rich in protein, butterfat, and Vitamins A and D. Try it on your own poodle. Give him one at bedtime—he'll love it.

BON APPÉTIT!

chapter 4

CARE AND TRAINING
OF A POODLE

O polished perturbation! Golden care!

HENRY IV

IT IS INCREDIBLE HOW MANY TIMES PEOPLE WILL ASK, "How do you bring up a poodle," or, on seeing a freshly clipped specimen, inquire, "Are poodles born that way?" A poodle is fed and brought up in the same manner as any other breed of dog, which is to say, the same manner in which a child is reared. The only difference is that, unlike any other breed, the poodle does not shed. His hair grows continually, and he has to be clipped periodically.

Now that the puppy has crossed your threshold, the first thing to do is to decide upon a name. This will depend largely on the fertility of your own imagination. Perhaps the poodle's appearance, a mannerism, or some cute little trick recently performed will suggest a name. When you decide, keep calling the puppy by the name, and he will recognize it within a very few days.

It will not be necessary to spend any large amount of money on equipment or accessories for the puppy. You need food and water dishes, a woolen or cotton throw for a bed, or, if the living quarters are large enough, a regular mattress bed. Make sure that the mattress is of cotton so that it may be readily washed, and that it is the zipper type, so that the filling may be taken out and changed. For mattress filling, cedar shavings may be used, or rubber foam which is vermin proof. Whether you use a throw or a bed, the point is to decide where you want him to sleep, place his bed there, let him know it is his bed and that this is where you expect him to sleep. Make sure that the location of the bed does not subject him to drafts.

Do not expect too much of him the first night or so. Most poodle puppies are so adaptable that they know, the moment they enter their new home, the place that belongs to them. But if the puppy has not had a great deal of human companionship he will be somewhat taken aback by all the attention being lavished upon him, the new home will have to be investigated; he will reconnoiter around the whole house, smelling every item and object, but he will settle down in a short time.

Acclimatization will be more rapid the more attention he receives. Most puppies whine a bit the first night, but this is forgivable since the surroundings are strange and they miss their brothers and sisters. Lee Smits, judge, breeder, and commentator, has a method that he feels is equivalent to a sedative. He insists that when a puppy goes to a new home the owner should wrap an alarm clock in a turkish towel and place it in the bed of the puppy. The muffled ticking of the clock resembles the heart beats of his brothers and sisters and thus makes him feel at home.

The puppy may not eat in a rugged manner the first day or so, but there is nothing to be alarmed about.

Housebreaking is a problem involving patience and perseverance. Although books galore have been written on the subject, there is no magic formula. Successful housebreaking depends upon many factors, all of which are individual to the dog and to you: how quickly he catches on, the time you arise, your own ability to teach, or that of your servants, and whether you live in the city or the country.

Cleanliness is instinctive with dogs, and housebreaking operations should begin immediately after the puppy enters the house. Bear in mind that a young puppy should go outdoors at least five times a day. If he cannot go outdoors, then "paper-break" him. Put paper down in the bathroom or kitchen. Watch him with an eagle eye, and the very split second you see him squat, pick him up and put him on the paper. Tell him a few times, "Go on the paper." If he does so, be sure to pet him and tell him what a good dog he is. (Dr. James R. Kinney even suggests that at this point the puppy be given a quarter for spending money.) Puppies take to paper-breaking quite easily. The place where the puppy will go is governed completely by his sense of smell; in order to insure his going on the paper a second time, and at all times thereafter, leave a small piece of soiled paper on the fresh paper that you put down. His sense of smell will guide him unerringly to this spot.

It is entirely unnecessary, as well as unproductive of results, to rub the puppy's nose in his mistake if he commits one on the rug or any other place besides the paper. It is advisable, however, to bring the puppy close to the scene of the crime, remind him that it is not cricket, and tell him that he must "go on the paper."

A lot of people prefer to send their puppies away for housebreaking, but results can never be guaranteed unless, upon returning home, the same routine as that set up by training is followed; the dog must go out at the same hours.

When you feel that the puppy is properly paper-trained, then you can gradually train him to go outdoors. He should be taken outside as early as possible in the morning and kept out until he does his duty, and he should always be taken out after feeding. Dogs love to fertilize the ground, and it will not take too long a time. At the age of six or seven months it is recommended that the puppy be taught to "speak" if he wants to go out. This he will do by going to the front door and giving a "woof."

A young puppy is not accustomed to wearing a collar or walking on a lead, and I do think breeders should pay more attention to this, and spend a few minutes a day lead-breaking puppies. Some of the better kennels do so now. Buy a leather collar and let him wear it around the house for a few days, but make sure the collar is not so large that it will slip over his head.

By no means put a harness type of collar on a poodle. These collars are for breeds whose respiratory action is unorthodox. A harness collar on a poodle will definitely interfere with the orderly bone growth and structure of the forelegs. Nature made the neck of the dog about the strongest part of its anatomy, so don't worry about a collar of the regulation type choking him or otherwise injuring his throat and neck.

After he has worn the collar a few days, buy a lead and take him walking. He probably will not care too much about the lead, for he is not used to this means of locomotion. You will have to pull him along with gentle, firm tugs, but in ten minutes' time he will realize it is much more decent to keep step with you than be dragged.

Never tie a puppy up in the house with his lead unless you are present to watch him. This represents a most unnatural act against his freedom, and he will bite through the lead. When the lead is not on him, keep it out of his reach or he will chew it.

Buy a few toys for the puppy—the brightest of days are those during which he is the busiest. Practically all toys are made of rubber, so be somewhat watchful over his tendency to chew off small bits and swallow them. Rubber tends to stick to the lining of the stomach. Leather toys are quite satisfactory.

Natural bones are important toys since they are a source of calcium and phosphorus. They are invaluable to puppies during their teething period, around four and a half months of age, if the right precautions are taken about their preparation. Shin bones with marrow content are especially good, but insist that the butcher saw the bone cleanly at both ends, leaving no jagged edge. A knuckle bone is also relished, and it assists in keeping tartar off the teeth. Most experts agree on the hazards of bone chewing; many say that the possibilities of slivers lodging in the throat outweigh the advantages. However, a bone is so natural a thing to a dog that few of us care to take the advice of experts. Steamed bone meal is recommended as a substitute for those who fear serious results from bone chewing.

The basic rules for the bringing up of a poodle puppy may be set forth as follows: give him (1) nourishing food regularly; (2) plenty of rest and sleep; (3) sufficient exercise and fresh air; (4) an abundance of affection and attention.

A puppy plays violently, and rest is probably more important than exercise. Mrs. George Putnam of the Puttencove Kennels in Massachusetts admonishes that proper exercise implies a "moderate amount of exercise." The puppy may be properly exercised without taking in too much territory. In the case of a young puppy the scampering around the house is sufficient. A ball or a leather strap will do wonders. Don't forget that it takes two to have a romp, and his playful spirit will help you forget the worries and cares of the day.

A poodle puppy does require an abundance of attention and companionship from people. Whoever said, "Affection lights a brighter flame than ever blazed by art," must have been thinking about poodles. This does not imply excessive pampering, but it means constant affection and care. Mrs. James M. Austin, Catawba Kennels, Westbury, Long Island, warns that a toy puppy requires an undue amount of personal affection and attention, although this should not be too difficult as the size invites cuddling.

There has always been, and probably always will be, disagreement as to when a puppy may be bathed. Many insist that a puppy should not have a bath until he is six months old, but there is no inviolable rule on the subject. It is perfectly all right to give a puppy a bath at three to four months of age, depending upon how and when he is bathed. Before that time the coat and skin are kept clean by daily brushing.

If the bathing is done in a beauty parlor where the drying out is by means of a hot dryer, no ill results could possibly follow. If it is done at home where there is no dryer, the puppy has to be rubbed vigorously with many dry towels and not allowed out after his bath. If the bathing is done in winter the important thing is to keep him out of drafts. Around three to four months of age the puppy is usually in his heavy puppy coat, and this takes more time to dry out than the short-coated breeds. With a heavy-coated puppy the best results are obtained by not using a brush. Squeeze the soap out of the coat and rinse well. Use a vinegar rinse if you like.

Joan Crawford relates: "Don't let anyone tell you a dog doesn't know when he's clipped and well groomed. Maybe it's because he was raised in a theatrical atmosphere, but my poodle Cliquot knows when he's trim and neat and has just been clipped and has had a bath. He prances around and shows off like any actor who knows he's making a good impression. When he's dirty and hasn't been properly groomed, he's depressed and keeps out of the way as though he doesn't want to be seen so badly got up."

The question is always asked, when may a poodle be clipped? The answer is, he may be clipped in any style at the age of three months. I have seen puppies clipped at the age of two months with no bad effects. Most people prefer mustache and beard on the face, but in the interest of cleanliness it is suggested the puppy have a clean face until such time as he eats without slobbering. Many do not recommend clipping at an early age because they feel the puppy looks more poodlish if left in the full puppy coat. However, considerations of brushing lead many to begin the clipping early in the puppy's life. This also sets the desired pattern as soon as possible.

Particular attention should be paid to the feet regardless of the type of clip. The hair between the pads, if allowed to grow unchecked, will curl and cause the toes to spread, which will result in sprawling, unpleasant-looking feet. This clipping should be done at least once a month. The nails, too, should be cut or filed once a month. Short hard nails are desirable and make for good feet, whereas long curly nails are unseemly and make for difficulty in walking. The hair in the ears should be attended to monthly.

The condition of a poodle's coat and skin generally reflects the state of his health. Vigorous brushing will do more than anything else to brace up the skin, eliminate the dead hair, and liven up the new growth. Brush him daily if you can, but you must brush him at least three times a week. Always brush against the growth of the hair. Brush his back toward the head and brush the legs upward. To do a thorough and efficient job, brush first with the growth of the hair and then finish by reversing the operation and brushing against the growth.

When brushing, work the coat out a little at a time and always brush away from you rather than toward you. At home the best results are obtained by training the puppy to lie on his side on the floor. For toys and miniatures, a natural bristle brush with a lightweight handle is the best. With a standard, the coat is somewhat heavier, and you may use a wire brush set in rubber. With a bristle brush the action should be with the wrist. With a wire brush, wrist action is not possible, and the tendency is to "dig" into the coat. The wire brush, when used properly, does not take out any more of the coat than should come out. Working the brush toward instead of away from the growth will surely result in digging out the hair unnecessarily rather than brushing it. And unless you are really expert with a comb, do not use one. The proper type of poodle comb, mentioned in the chapter on clipping, does not have a handle because a handle furnishes the temptation to dig and pull. A comb should be used only for fluffing the hair. I have seen many a tail pompom ruined by digging with a comb.

The coat of a poodle puppy is soft and silky and will continue to be so until he is almost a year old. Unless he has an exceptionally frizzy coat, a puppy is shown in his natural coat or puppy clip, because there is not sufficient texture for any other style of clip. Many poodle owners who have their puppies cut in the Dutch or Sporting Clip are greatly disappointed when the coat does not stand out as it does on mature dogs. If you are interested in a good harsh coat, then the vital age is about seven months, when the mature hair starts to grow in and take the place of the silky coat. This is the age when the puppy should be scissored or clipped down to the Kennel Clip. I have seen several instances of poodles nine or ten months of age with long coats, not properly taken care of, the mature hair so matted and gnarled that the only thing to do was clip it off down to the skin.

You will invariably run into pessimists who tell you that the country is the only place for a dog. However, the very nature of the dog is such that he wants to be with you and is unconcerned as to where you live. He is far happier in a hut or a cold-water tenement with good food, a few rompings, and the companionship of his master than on a thousand-acre estate where he has to fend for himself. The cement and brick sidewalks of the city do his feet far more good than the soft sands of the beach or the grassy lawns of the country. And the city dog lives from two to three years longer than the country dog, according to studies undertaken by veterinarians.

With the advent of hot weather, special thought must be given to the comfort of your poodle. A dog's skin has no pores, and he perspires only through his tongue, and to a limited extent through the pads of his feet. Although the poodle is not so susceptible to sunburn as the short-haired dogs, he should be kept out of the direct rays of the sun. The coat nature provided him with acts as insulation against heat as well as cold. Whether indoors or out, he will find the place coolest for him.

In the summertime cut down sharply on the amount of meat in his diet. If he is at the beach or lake for the summer, he will probably spend most of the time in the water. As soon as he is finished for the day, rub him vigorously with a dry towel, particularly the legs and feet, because wet eczema may result from failing to be dried out rapidly. If he is constantly in salt water, watch out for "salt-water" eyes and wipe his eyes out thoroughly with boric acid solution. Constant riding in a car with his head out of the window may cause eye trouble, for the wind carries tiny particles of dust which may set up an irritation. Wash out with solution of boric acid.

Many poodles dry out too much in the summertime, and their skin becomes parched and scaly. Their skin, exposed to the sun, requires, if anything, more oils. Use more wheat-germ oil in the summer as well as cutting down on meat. Also, a lotion containing menthol and lanolin will have a cooling and softening effect on the skin. Don't fall for the old gag of putting a block of sulphur in the drinking water and feel that this will thin out the blood and tend to keep him cooler. Sulphur is not soluble in water and does not have any such effect on the blood, but colloidal sulphur injected intravenously is efficacious with minor skin eruptions that occur in the heat of the summer.

As for the winter, the thing to avoid in the case of a puppy is cold wind. Cold weather he will probably love, but a cold wind is a puppy's worst enemy. It chills him through and lowers his resistance.

Let them gambol in the snow—they love it, although with a puppy avoid overindulgence. Some poodles I know are perfect prognosticators of snow; they sniff it in the air long before the weather man predicts it, and when it comes they want to romp with reckless abandon. It's not a bad idea for you to go out with him, for the sport and to watch that he doesn't overdo. When he comes back into the house, dry his feet carefully with a towel. Make sure there is no caking of the snow into ice between the pads of his feet.

Some people like to furnish their dogs with overcoats or sweaters for walking in the winter. If the dog is confined in a steam-heated home or apartment the greater portion of the day, overcoat protection against a chilling cold is prudent, though cold weather is good for the coat. Ordinarily poodles, being of a hardy breed, require no overcoat except their own, and any shivering or fright of the cold is probably due to lack of circulation.

You should have available at all times a thermometer with which to take the dog's temperature rectally. The normal temperaure of a dog is 102 degrees, and although a cool, moist nose is a fairly good indication of good health, it is not infallible. If the temperature is over 102 degrees, a veterinarian should be consulted. If your dog becomes sick, eliminate hospitalization if possible. He will be far happier at home in his normal surroundings with your comforting words.

I frequently feel that we in the United States are backward in not recognizing the dog for what he is. In England and on the Continent where an older civilization prevails, dogs run and play unleashed in all open places and on the beaches. They go to theaters, restaurants, on buses and trains, and are considered a necessary adjunct of living. In the United States many restaurants and most hotels have a prohibition against dogs, although personally I would not stay at a hotel or go to a restaurant where I could not take a dog, and our beaches and parks are closed to dogs unless they are leashed. People should demand that some open spaces be set aside in which their dogs can exercise. As usual there are two sides to the question, and it is regrettably true that our dogs are not so well behaved, let us say, as the dogs of England and the Continent.

It is necessary that you train your puppy, and by training I mean education that imparts character and discipline, education that establishes the pattern of correct behavior so that he will acquire the proper house and street manners. This training should be undertaken when the puppy is about five months of age. As Virgil pointed out:

"Thus training is of great importance in the early years." The susceptibility of the poodle puppy to early training was pointed out in *The Sportsman's Cabinet*, published in London in 1803: "It is no matter of surprise that he should, even from infancy, be more susceptible of, and subservient to, inculcations of obedience. . . . Even in puppy-hood [he] displays an eager desire to be employed in office of domestic amusement, in proof of which eager propensity, a variety of such useful utensils as are generally deposited on the floor frequently undergo speedy mutilation little short of destruction. . . . It is during this inclination to bustle and business that their scholastic inculcation should commence; when their aptitude for instruction, and ready tendency to obedience will be found not only to go hand in hand with the attention bestowed, but very far exceed, in progress and proficiency, the most sanguine expectations."

There is nothing more excruciating to a dog-lover than the sight of somebody walking down the street with a dog dragging after him, lurching from right to left, interfering with pedestrian traffic, getting tangled up with other dogs. Nothing furnishes dog-haters with better propaganda than the untrained dog performing his toilet on the sidewalk or in some other improper place. Order is still heaven's first law, and dogs, like human beings, find themselves in trouble only when disobedient.

When you start to train your puppy at the age of four or five months, the use of a metal chain slip collar, sometimes called a choke collar, is not recommended, and is, as a matter of fact, unnecessary. Such a collar is for use later, when the dog goes into obedience training. Now the ordinary leather collar is enough.

The first item in training is teaching the puppy to walk on a lead properly or to "heel." The handle of the lead should be carried in your right hand, and your left hand should hold the lead in the center. The puppy should be on your left. When he lurches forward, give the lead a sharp jerk with your left hand, not too severely, and at the same time say the word "heel." The object is for the dog to walk quietly by your left side, not straining at his collar or leading ahead at any time. Try to do this ten or fifteen minutes a day, but do it at the same time and the same place. You can do it in the house if you like. No play or fun should be allowed during this fifteen-minute period. Your voice should be decisive and commanding in quality. That does not mean it should be harsh, exciting, or explosive. Continue the firmness until your return to the house and then, of course, you will tell him what a good dog he has been and give him a biscuit or two. To a dog, a biscuit represents what is known in capitalistic countries as the "profit incentive."

At five months of age these lessons might be undertaken twice a week, for ten to fifteen minutes a day. As the puppy grows older, increase to three or four times a week for twenty to thirty minutes. No useful result will be accomplished if such training work is begun prior to five months of age, and even at five months of age do not expect too much of the puppy, and do not become impatient or lose your temper.

The poodle has a quality that scientists call motivation. This means responsiveness, in that he wants to do what he is told to do, but you have to know what to tell him and how to convey it. A puppy's mind is active and acquisitive but has none too great a power of retention. Over seventy years ago T. H. Joyce commented: "Like a child, however, he requires careful handling, for while he is easily trained, he is exceptionally sensitive and is far more efficiently taught when treated as a sensible being than as a mere quadrupedal automaton, and will learn twice as quickly if his master can make him understand the reason for performing that task."

Miss Blanche Saunders, noted obedience authority of the Carillon Kennels, has written an excellent book entitled *Training You to Train Your Dog*. The title is apropos. The dog is there, ready, willing, and eager to learn and absorb. You are the one that has to be trained in order to train him. Miss Saunders wants you to know that "the poodle's keen intelligence makes training him a pleasure. His quickness to learn is almost uncanny, for once he is shown what to do he responds with enthusiasm. By forming correct habits from puppyhood, severe corrections may be avoided later on at an age when it might have a bad effect on the dog. The poodle breed is unusually sensitive and a harsh tone of voice will often cause a poodle to remain dejected and low in spirit for long periods of time. Even a slight correction should immediately be followed by kind words if one is to retain the natural gaiety that is typical of the breed.

"Early schooling will lead to a better understanding between the owner and his dog. This early schooling should include the basic obedience exercises in elementary form, such as walking on a lead, sitting and lying down on command, coming when called and staying when told. However, this must be accomplished in a gentle manner. The poodle puppy will obey easily and willingly if the owner is patient and not too demanding.

"The poodle owner will get more enjoyment from his dog and better results in training if he will but stop to analyze the temperament of the breed. One outstanding characteristic is that the poodle prefers to follow a leader rather than take the initiative; in other words, he can be led anywhere but not pushed. Being anxious to please his owner, he will cooperate in every way until unwanted force is applied, then he will suddenly lose interest.

"Since the poodle is a born clown and natural showoff, he does not take his early training seriously so cannot always be relied upon. Because the breed has been used so long and extensively in the entertainment world, the poodle loves applause, nor is he past taking advantage of people, if he is to profit by their lapses. He must therefore be handled firmly so as to leave no doubt as to who is master, yet handled in a kind and understanding way.

"The poodle bores easily. He is continually looking for new interests, excitement, new worlds to conquer. When there is a lack of entertainment, he will invent and provide his own amusement and then laugh at the results. Having a positive sense of humor, he expects his owner to have it as well. As a watch dog he gives warning and attacks only if necessary, or when trained to. The poodle is not a troublemaker unless forced to defend himself, at which time he puts up a good fight to the end. He gets along with other dogs. His patience, loyalty, and faithfulness make him an ideal companion. All this is why the poodle owner has not one poodle in a lifetime, but many."

During the two or three times a week you are training your puppy to heel, do not attempt any other type of training. One thing at a time. When he appears to respond fairly well to your heel commands, you may take up with him the matter of "sit"—sitting down. This may be started at home, although outdoors is better—free from distractions and toys. When he is in a standing position, and don't forget to put on your firm voice, tell him "sit" and at the same moment put your left hand on his back between the hips and the base of his tail and gently press him down to a sitting position. Repeat this a few times so that he can associate the word "sit" with the position he is to assume. When he catches on, walk away from him a few steps. He probably will get up and follow you; you will have to go back and repeat the instruction. After a few lessons he will know what is required of him and will remain in a sitting position until you tell him "all right." While he is sitting, walk around him three or four times and see to it that he remains seated. As the lessons progress, walk farther away from him, telling him at all times to "sit." These lessons should be carried on for ten or fifteen minutes a day, three or four times a week, independent of any other teachings.

When you feel he is ready for the next lesson you should start in on the "stay." Put him in a sitting position and, walking away from him or walking around him, tell him to sit, which he will do, and then use the word "stay." Repeat the word a few times so that he may catch on to what you mean. Be patient, of course, and do not use any other word or words, except possibly to tell him what a good dog he is. Walk about five or ten feet away from him, repeating the word "stay." Make him remain in that position for a minute or two, and, naturally, as the training progresses and he grows older, he will be able to sit for an even longer period of time, and you might try going out of sight for one or two minutes.

For a dog to come when called is quite important to an owner. If a dog is properly trained along this line you will obviate dog fights and be prepared for unforeseen situations. The best method is to take the puppy outdoors and tie him to one end of a clothesline about fifteen or twenty feet in length. When he reaches the end of it, wait until he sits down and faces you, as he probably will. Then direct him to "come" or "come here," and at the same time pull the line toward you and make him come to you. He will wriggle and squirm and object somewhat, but pull him to a position in front of you. He must associate immediate movement toward you when he hears the word "come." When he is in front of your feet, pat his head, and praise him. Repeat this five or six times, and do the same thing two or three times a week. In the course of two or three weeks you will find instantaneous response and no clothesline will be needed. But, it must be remembered, these lessons are preliminary and have to be carried out later on in obedience training.

The matter of teaching him how to "fetch" is not too difficult. This is of course preceded by his carrying articles in his mouth. It is the most natural thing in the world for a poodle to carry; indeed, he is never so happy as when he is prancing around with something in his mouth, albeit the beginning of this business is usually with a new slipper. In teaching him to carry, place a rubber or wooden dumbbell in his mouth and say "carry." If he drops it, put it back in his mouth— he will catch on to the idea. After he has learned to carry for some time, take him outdoors, throw the dumbbell some distance away, and tell him to "fetch." For the first few lessons he may not be willing to drop the object at your feet and you may have to teach him to "drop," but in future lessons he will deposit the retrieved object at your feet when you tell him to. The teaching to "drop" is necessary because his inquisitiveness plus his eagerness to carry will lead him to pick up and carry undesirable objects, including moldy bones and contaminated items.

Poodles are just so glad to see you that they cannot resist jumping on you as a greeting. This is simple to cure. When the puppy jumps, bring your right knee up sharply against his chest bone, and at the moment of impact say "down." Do it quickly so that the puppy will not know the force emanates from you. It is a sure cure and after three or four solid impacts, provided they are firm enough, the puppy loses his desire to jump up. Another method is to step briskly on one of the back feet at the first moment of jumping. He will associate discomfort with jumping up and will not try it many times thereafter. With standards, however, I have difficulty with this method; they are so smart and they stand back so far you cannot reach their back feet.

The preliminary training discussed above should not be confused with obedience training. Obedience training represents a college education and should not be undertaken until the dog is about a year old. In some instances dogs may be accepted for obedience training if they are under one year, provided their preliminary education indicates such precocity as to qualify them to enter college at an early age. Obedience training is carried on with a slip chain collar, sometimes called a choke collar. No matter what anyone thinks, it does not hurt. The neck, as has been stated before, is the strongest part of the dog, and no harm has ever resulted from this metal collar, worn loose around the dog's neck, if used properly. That is why you have to go to college with the dog and learn at the same time. The collar should be used only for obedience training since he must associate the wearing of it with his training period.

The matter of obedience training and competition should be of special interest to poodle owners as poodles have always excelled in this type of work. The obedience work going on in the United States today is credited originally to Mrs. Whitehouse Walker. In 1931 she became enamored of the breed, which resulted in the founding of the Carillon Kennels and the Poodle Club of America in the same year.

The obedience work being done with poodles in England by Mrs.

Grace Boyd, particularly with King Leo of Piperscroft, attracted Mrs. Walker's attention. Having an abiding faith in the intelligence of poodles, she felt that they would be most adept in such work in the United States and thus exhibit their brains as well as their beauty. In 1934 she spent many months in England, studying the obedience tests there, and upon her return wrote many articles urging adoption in the United States. She enthusiastically spoke, preached, and argued, and finally formed the Obedience Test Club of New York. The rules and regulations for obedience work drawn up by that club were adopted in 1936 by the American Kennel Club, which granted permission for obedience tests to be carried on at regular dog shows.

In the early part of 1936 the first obedience test at a regular A.K.C. dog show was held in Westchester County, New York. At this show the first three places were taken by poodles. During the first year of such tests, 28 dogs representing eight breeds received titles. Of these 28 dogs, 17 were poodles. Of the 28 dogs, 25 received the C.D. (Companion Dog) title and 3—all poodles—received the C.D.X. (Companion Dog Excellent) title. The first dog in the United States to win all three American Kennel Club titles, C.D., C.D.X., and U.D. (Utility Dog), was a poodle named Carillon Epreuve, owned by Mrs. Walker, handled and trained by Blanche Saunders.

If your poodle has done well in obedience training, you may want to put him in competition at regular dog shows. If so, Miss Blanche Saunders points out: "Such obedience competition should not be attempted until the poodle has matured physically as well as mentally. If the actual training is completed when he is two or three years old and perfection in his work gradually attained over a longer period of time, the efforts will be more satisfying and the results will be a credit to both the owner and the dog."

The purpose of obedience trials is to demonstrate the usefulness of a dog as the companion and guardian of man. The trials are held under the regulations and standards of the American Kennel Club. The various classes and titles conferred may be described as follows:

NOVICE—*Class A*

This is for dogs which have not won the title C.D. (Companion Dog). Dogs in this class must be exhibited by owner or member of immediate family.

NOVICE—*Class B*

This class is for dogs who have not won the C.D. Dogs in this class may be handled by either an amateur or professional.

In the novice class there are six tests:

Heel on leash	35 points
Stand for examination	30 points
Heel free	45 points
Recall	30 points
Long sit	30 points
Long down	30 points

This represents a possible maximum of 200 points. In order to secure the C.D. title, a dog must receive more than fifty per cent of the available points in each of the six tests and a total score of 170 or more in three separate obedience trials.

OPEN—*Class A*

For dogs which have won the title C.D. and must be exhibited by owner or member of immediate family. No dog with the title of C.D.X. can be entered in this class.

OPEN—*Class B*

For dogs which have won the title of C.D. and may be handled by either amateur or professional. Dog that has won the title C.D.X. may be entered.

In this open class there are seven tests:

Heel free	40 points
Drop on recall	30 points
Retrieve on flat	25 points
Retrieve over high jump	35 points
Broad jump	20 points
Long sit	25 points
Long down	25 points

There is a possible maximum of 200 points, and the title C.D.X. (Companion Dog Excellent) may be conferred if the dog scores more than fifty per cent of the available points in each of the seven tests and achieves a total score of 170 or more in three obedience trials.

UTILITY CLASS

For dogs that have won the title C.D.X. Handlers, trainers, and kennel employees may handle. There are seven tests:

Scent discrimination, Article 1   20 points
Scent discrimination, Article 2   20 points
Scent discrimination, Article 3   20 points
Seek back   30 points
Signal exercise   35 points
Directed jumping   40 points
Group examination   35 points

The possible maximum score is 200, and the title U.D. (Utility Dog) will be conferred if the dog receives fifty per cent of the available points in each of the seven tests and a total score of 170 or more in three obedience trials.

TRACKING TEST

These tests are not held indoors or at dog shows. The title T.D. (Tracking Dog) may be used after the name of a dog if two judges certify that the test in which at least three dogs have appeared was passed. In the event a dog holds both titles of Utility Dog and Tracking Dog, these titles may be combined as U.D.T., that is, Utility Dog Tracker.

You will find that the poodle is a seasoned traveler—by land, sea, and air. Railroad travel is somewhat of a nuisance as most roads require dogs to ride in the baggage car, and when no baggage car is on the train they are not usually accepted. Where Pullman accommodations are available on the train you may take the dog with you, provided you have a drawing room, compartment, or private room. The Pullman regulations are as follows: "Dogs . . . may be taken into private room accommodations in Pullman cars but only when carried in baskets or other containers. They may not be taken into or out of the car in any other manner." The word "container" is so general that in the case of toys and miniatures I have found a paper bag sufficient to carry a dog through the gate and into the Pullman car.

Up-to-date ocean liners have a space set aside for dogs, and they even have their own private deck. Although the rule is that a dog may not be taken into a cabin, you will sometimes find a warmhearted steward who will overlook his presence there.

Travel by air presents a difficult problem as there is no uniformity in the rules. If, however, you are shipping your dog outside the state without accompanying him, he will have to travel on a cargo plane, that is, a plane that carries only freight and no passengers. Have no qualms about this, however, for the probability is that the pilot will have him up in the cockpit as company.

In shipping a dog via freight, whether by railroad or plane, the rule is that the dog shall be boxed or crated in such a manner as to prevent escape and to insure safe transportation. Further, some states require a health certificate if a dog is to be shipped there. These states are Connecticut, Florida, Georgia, Iowa, Kansas, Maine, Michigan, Minnesota, New Jersey, North Dakota, South Dakota, Pennsylvania, Utah, Vermont, and Wisconsin. The veterinarian's certificate should set forth that the dog was recently vaccinated against rabies, furnish a description of the dog, and attest that he is free from any infectious or communicable disease. When shipping a dog by plane, even though it is being shipped to a state which does not require such a health certificate, it is the better part of wisdom to secure such a certificate, as there is no guarantee the plane will not be grounded in a state where the certificate requirement is rigidly enforced.

The desirable thing is, of course, for the dog to travel with you on the same plane, and most of the airlines allow this provided he is crated properly, is within the weight limit, and rides not in the passenger section but as excess baggage. The following companies will allow this: American, Capital, Challenger, Chicago and Southern, Colonial, Eastern, Mid-Continent, Monarch, National, Northeast, Piedmont, Pioneer, Southwest, and TWA. The following lines will take dogs only as cargo equipment, not on passenger flights: Inland, Northwest, and United. Braniff, Robinson, and Western are not equipped to handle dogs on any flights. These listings are subject to change, and should be verified with the airline company beforehand. Also, the listings pertain only to those passenger flights which are not stratospheric. Up until recently practically all of the airline companies have refused to take dogs on planes which were pressurized, but this prohibition has been lifted by some companies.

chapter 5

HOW TO CLIP
AND TYPES OF CLIPS

A poodle once towed me along,
But always we came to one harbour;
To keep his curls smart,
And shave his hind part,
He constantly called on a barber.
TOM HOOD

THERE ARE ONLY THREE STYLES OF CLIP RECOGNIZED FOR show by the Poodle Club of America and the American Kennel Club. These are the English Saddle, the Continental, and the Puppy. This means that poodles must be clipped in this manner and style in order to be exhibited in a show officially recognized by the American Kennel Club.

The first two styles are termed traditional; that is, poodles were clipped in these styles many years ago when they were used for fowling. It may amaze more than a few to know that the Continental, for example, is at least three hundred years old. In Germany and France it was the custom, arising out of necessity, to "shave the hind parts" in order to achieve swiftness and lightness in the water. As early as 1621 Gervase Markham wrote: "Now, for the cutting or shaving him from the navill downeward or backward, it is two wayes will to be allowed of, that is, for summer hunting or for the water; because these Water Dogges naturally are ever most laden with haires on the hinder parts, Nature as it were labouring to defend that part most, which is continually to bee employed in the most extremity, and because the hinder parts are ever deeper in water than the fore parts. . . ."

And Edward C. Ash, writing about the eighteenth-century poodle, said: "The clipping of the coat, as already stated, was a matter of considerable antiquity, for the earliest illustrations of poodles show the animal with the hinder portion of the coat removed. But in several sixteenth-century manuscripts are roughly executed designs of dogs shaven on a similar plan to the description given above."

The bracelets on the legs and the pompom on the tail are not whimsical fashion notes. When we read the literature of the eighteenth and nineteenth centuries we are constantly reminded of the suffering of human beings from aches and pains about the joints. Rheumatism appeared to be the fashionable malady of the day. The German and French fowlers frequently commented on the dogged persistence of the poodle in not coming out of the water if a single duck were missing. Some complained that their poodle remained in the cold water all night long until he found and brought in the missing duck. The bracelets on the legs, therefore, were left in order to protect the joints against rheumatism. The pompom on the tail was functional: it was a periscopic signal, enabling one to follow the course of the dog in the water. In the Continental clip pompoms are left on the hip bones, and this again was a precaution to protect the joints.

When the poodle was becoming popular in England around 1830 the English did not fancy the Continental clip, not understanding its functional purpose. Most of the writers of that period would not believe that the poodle could withstand the rigors of the English winter, and we know there was much complaining about the ague, chills, fever, and rheumatism. Barton, in *The Dog*, published in 1848, had a different type of complaint. He warned: "They are very handsome dogs when the toilet is properly attended to, but it is an expensive business to keep a poodle trimmed to the height of fashion." Lee said that the custom of the continental fowlers in shaving their poodles was not quite understood in England, where there was so much cold water, mud, and slush in the winter. In 1886 Walsh wrote that the French and Dutch fowlers had the "strange habit of clipping him also over the face in such a manner as to leave him very distinctly a moustache and an imperiale, which ornaments give the dog a very comical and cunning appearance." In Germany the writers insisted that a mustache of "aldermanic proportions" was just the thing. In *The Black Poodle* by F. Anstey in 1884, we read that the poodle was "shaved in the sham-lion fashion, which is considered for some mysterious reason to improve a poodle, but the barber had left sundry little tufts of hair which studded his haunches capriciously."

Stables, in 1890, wrote: "The face is clipped bare with the exception of a daft pantaloon-like pair of eyebrows and a pair of moustachios and a small goatee. Then the body abaft the ribs are clipped bare, as well as the belly and the thighs and legs, with the following exceptions; a pair of epaulettes are left on the top of the rump and a fringe of hair around the hocks. The fore legs are clipped with the exception of a fringe of hair around the knees, zu-lu fashion."

Dalziel in 1870 pleaded for an end of the "vulgar fancies of the dog barber" by which the poodle was denuded of coat in a variety of fantastic fashions and a "large, ugly tassel is left to dangle from the end of the stump." He objected to a "three-parts shaved off a long, thick-coated dog" and recommended that one-third be shaved.

The English devised their own style of clip, known today as the English Saddle. Firm in their belief that the poodle could not bear up under the English winter, they did not shave the hind part off entirely in continental fashion but allowed about one-half inch of hair to remain on the hind part. This they called the "pack." Out of the pack they fashioned a saddle from which the clip derives its name. The saddle is merely a circular shaped depression clipped out of the pack, on both sides of the dog, at a point between the ribs and the loin. The saddle accentuates the pack, also the ruff. The mustache was retained. Maxtee said: "The face should be left bare except for a moustache and imperiale," and von Bensheim later mentioned that "a good moustache must be left." Gradually, however, the mustache went into disfavor not only for sanitary reasons but because it was impossible to judge properly the muzzle, nose, mouth, chin, and flews. Today the rule for exhibition in the United States requires the face to be clipped clean.

The English also changed the location of the hip pompoms in the Continental clip. Instead of centering them on the hip bones, they transferred them to a location between the bottom rib and the haunch bones. They called them rosettes, and in trimming they usually scissored them flat, whereas in the United States we scissor so as to leave a smooth convex effect.

The French fanciers, individualists always, did not adhere to form but commenced shaving the backs of their poodles in a variety of dreambeset and imaginative styles, in some instances going so far as to embellish the hind part with the coat of arms of the owner, or perhaps shaving out the ace of clubs. Patterns could be sought showing new ideas in shaving, and poodle barbers, the forerunners of our present poodle beauty-shop stylists, set themselves up in business in street stalls in Paris. During the nineteenth century the clipping operation was termed "shaving," as the only implement available for the work was the straight-edge barber razor.

The *New York Daily Tribune* took note of the French poodle situation in 1893 and commented: "They are the favorites of the Parisian belles. Female poodle barbers are now an institution in Paris, for they make the Parisian poodles. They take a poodle and when they are through with him he is trimmed and decorated in the most elaborate and approved styles. These barbers cut off some of the hair, so that what is left is in the form of rosettes, bangs and other designs. The dog, after the artist barber is through with him, looks like a strange animal. The Parisian belle is different from the American girl, for instead of leaving her pet at home she takes him wherever she goes and has him decked in fancy costumes made of material to match her own gown. Sometimes the dogs are adorned with jewelled bangles and ribbons."

It is probably true that most poodle owners prefer the Dutch Cut for the miniature, the Sporting Clip for the standard, and are most indignant when apprised that their poodles may not be shown in such clips. On the other hand, most poodle breeders are purists and feel that such unorthodox clips are a monstrosity. It is utilitarianism versus beauty and never the twain shall meet.

The fact is, the decision to bar from the ring all unorthodox clips is not based on whim or caprice. The traditional clips show the poodle in its historically correct and functional style. The other styles are outlawed for show for the honorable and valid reason that a poodle clipped in any other manner cannot be efficiently and honestly judged. For example, how can cow hocks be determined in the Sporting Clip or flat feet detected when a poodle is left with terrier feet? How can the coat be judged when there is no coat, and what about carriage and gait? Countenance is the reflection of the soul, and the poodle expression must always be present, but where is it when the ears are clipped bare? Many other additional reasons could be pointed out. That is one side of the question. But what about the joy of having your poodle clipped in any manner you desire, to please your own taste and fancy but subject at all times, of course, to the conformation of the dog's body? You will have to experiment with many types of clips, coiffure, and variations thereof before you achieve just the right combination that will bring out all the innate pertness, poise, and gaiety of your dog—something to match his personality, and yours too.

In order to clip and groom you must have a table. It should have an appropriately large surface covered with a rubber mat or rough plastic to prevent the dog from slipping. If you are doing whites, a black or dark table surface is preferable. If doing blacks, a white covering may help your eye. Generally speaking, the table should be from thirty-two to thirty-four inches in height but to insure your comfort it can vary according to your own height. Extend your arms out in front of you. The fingertip point should be at the level of the middle of the dog. If you are doing standards, the table will be lower than one for clipping toys. The table must be steady so as not to quiver, and should have ample drawer space for your tools and equipment so you will not have to fumble around for them. Light is most important, and the better artists have, in addition to proper overhead light, a set of side lights, in order to illuminate better the bracelets and the pantaloons. Although it does appear that expert clippers are born and not made, time and experience will enable you to achieve more than a modicum of success if you are not near a beauty parlor. And don't forget Michelangelo's classic retort to the woman who chided him for paying too much attention to a few strands of hair: "Trifles make perfection and perfection is no trifle."

Next, you require an electric clipping machine which will operate on either AC or DC power, with at least one extra removable head to substitute immediately should the first become too hot. Care must be taken not to overuse the machine at one working. Keep feeling it, and when it becomes too hot, transfer to a new head. You will want a secure place to hold the clippers while they are not being used, and a small box on the side of the wall would be appropriate. Also, the electrical outlet should be about four feet up from the floor, in order to prevent tripping over the cord while you are working.

There are various types of blades, running from very fine to coarse. They bear numbers 40, 30, 15, 7, and 5. The No. 40 blade is extremely fine, is for surgical work only and not for amateurs. The No. 30 blade is fairly fine and is frequently used in clipping poodles for show; however, it cuts too close for most people interested in clipping for non-show purposes. Also, it is probably just a bit too fine for the face, feet, and tail. However, you should have a blade of this type as you will find it just the proper thing, with a steady hand, of course, for cleaning up the hair on the edge of the lips and for trimming the outside edge of the ear in a clip that requires the ears to be clean of hair. The No. 15 blade is the all-purpose one; with this you can clip the face, feet, tail, and body. The best results with this blade are obtained when you clip *against* the growth of the hair. A slightly coarser blade is the No. 10, which you should have. This blade operates best when used to clip *with* the growth of the hair. If you do not care for a closely clipped face and body, then you should use the No. 10 blade, working it always away from the muzzle and toward the tail. Coarser yet are blades No. 7 and No. 5. These are for those who do not care for a sleek body appearance and prefer a rougher coat.

You will also want a comb. Buy one specially designed for poodle work. It should have teeth that are round and long and widely spaced. But before you buy a comb, remember that it is for professionals only, and far too many poodle coats are ruined through its injudicious use. Mats in the coat cannot be taken out with a comb, but only by brushing and working them out with your fingers. A comb is used only for fluffing out the hair, not for taking the coat out.

One or two pairs of sharp barber scissors are necessary and of course a brush. For standards, a most satisfactory brush is the type with wire pins set in rubber, thereby giving the pins flexibility. To hold this brush properly, lay it on the table with the pins down, place your thumb on the back of the handle—that is, the part that faces up—then put the fingers on the other side of the handle and lift the brush up. Grasping the brush in this manner necessitates brushing away from you. When you grasp the handle as you would a knife or fork and use it so that you brush toward you, you will dig out the coat.

For miniatures and toys, although the coats of the former can be just as frizzy as the standard's, most people prefer a bristle brush. A brush of genuine natural Siberian bristle is the perfect instrument. Make sure that the handle is of light weight as it will be less tiring. A bristle has tiny microscopic fibers that run off the main stem. These fibers are the cleansing agents—they clean out all dust particles. With too soft a brush the coat will not receive the proper amount of invigoration.

You will also need nail clippers and file. Nails must be attended to at least once a month since poodle carriage cannot be maintained with long, curving, neglected nails. Within the nail there is the quick, live flesh which should not be cut into as it will bleed. It may be seen from the underneath portion of the nail. Cut as close to the quick as possible but not into it. With standards, the nails are large enough so that a file can be used. In filing, draw the file only in one direction, and that is downward.

So many people marvel at the patience and docility of the poodle while undergoing his toilette. He will stand quietly for as long a time as necessary to complete the grooming without tiring, complaining, or becoming fidgety. Obviously nature, in creating the necessity for such treatments, gave the poodle the forebearance and fortitude with which to endure it, although I doubt whether "endure" is the proper word. There is nothing harsh or prolonged about the treatment; as a matter of fact, I know few poodles who disdain or dislike it. A. H. Trapman said in his *Man's Best Friend* that the poodle endures the constant brushing and combing necessary for keeping his coat in order because he is conceited. I have seen many girl poodles promenade home after a beauty-parlor treatment with such a pretentious manner and air of affection that I wonder whether it is an exhibition of pride or down-right ostentation; but never conceit, a vice possessed only by us human beings. Sir Walter Scott said that God, in giving us the dog for our pleasant companionship, "invested him with a noble nature incapable of deceit"; and "A dog," says one of the English poets, "is an honest creature and I am a friend to dogs." Poodle owners will prefer von Bensheim, who, in analyzing the reactions of a poodle while being groomed, exclaimed: "The tenderness of a beloved hand, the slightest touch of which fills him with happiness."

If you are going to bathe and clip the dog, the procedure is to do the main part of the clipping before the bath. Start out with a brushing, to free the coat of mats and snares. If this is not done, the soap will imbed itself in the mats and harden them. Have the dog lie on his side and brush toward the feet; hold the unbrushed hair down with your free hand and work out a small amount of hair at a time. When he is fairly well brushed—although this is preliminary to the main brushing that comes after the bath—you may start to clip. The face is usually done first. There is no definite rule on this and many prefer to do the feet first as the dog may not like a warm machine on his feet and pull away. The tail is the most sensitive part, and on whites and on young dogs that have not undergone much clipping, I would say do the tail first and immediately after finishing rub on some hand lotion or boric acid powder. When you have completed the main job of clipping, there will be many small touches yet to be done. Leave this finishing up till after the bath.

There is no question but that bathing has a tendency to soften up the coat, so that if you are contemplating exhibiting you probably will not bathe him. There are many excellent items on the market that are substitutes for a water bath. Frequent brushings with the right type of bristle brush clean the coat. If you have a white poodle you can use a cleansing power, well rubbed in; but it must be entirely brushed out, for if any traces of it remain, your dog may be disqualified in the ring. If you have a black or a brown, you can use dry cleaning pads or a type of liquid cleaner.

If you are bathing with water, the first thing to do is to stuff the ears with absorbent cotton and put a drop of mineral oil in each eye. Start the bathing process at the tail and wash toward the muzzle, leaving the latter until the last. If there is any evidence of fleas, the very first thing to do is to work up a lather of suds and ring them around the dog's neck, because when bathing starts these creatures scamper toward the head and ears, where they cleverly conceal themselves. Use any type of soap—shampoo, soap flakes, or jelly. All soap, of course, has some degree of causticity.

You can use one of the new detergents on the market; they are most efficacious in removing the dirt and are not toxic. If your dog is in show cut, you should wash the ruff by squeezing, since a brush might injure the coat; otherwise a brush may be used all over the body. A rice-root brush is good for scrubbing, provided the bristles are not packed together too tightly.

Wash the head and face last of all. To rinse the head, take a pan of water in one hand, and with the other reach under the dog's throat and take hold of both ears, pressing them tightly against the head so that no rinse water can get into the ears. Then tilt the head slightly upward and rinse. Another way, in case you are more worried about the eyes than the ears, is to cover the eyes with one hand while rinsing with the other. In order to rid the coat of every particle of soap, a vinegar rinse should be used. If the presence of fleas, lice, or ticks is apparent or suspected, you should use a solution to eliminate the vermin. Fleas may be eliminated by almost any of the commercial solutions being sold today. The same is true of lice, although with lice it is necessary to repeat the solution rinse about five or six days after the first because the initial rinse will not affect the eggs which will soon hatch out. Ticks are most difficult to kill; to do a thoroughly lethal job, use a rinse solution containing stabilized rotenoids or a U.S. government-approved type of chlordane.

If you are bathing a black dog and his coat is not a true inky black, then use, in addition, a rinse prepared with a small amount of bluing; this will make his coat appear blacker. A white dog may also be given a bluing rinse. Some who own the lighter shades of browns demand a bluing rinse since it leaves something of a mauve cast.

After bathing, the dog should be allowed to shake. Then take as much of the water as possible off with a large absorbent bath towel, and dry him out under a hot dryer if possible. There are available small hand dryers, which are satisfactory, and some even use a vacuum cleaner in reverse. For those who do not have a dryer, there is nothing to do but to use plenty of towels and keep on rubbing.

When you become really proficient in your clipping and treatment of coat and skin, you will want what is called a rake-comb. This is a gadget devised for raking out a poodle's coat just before it becomes thoroughly dry. It eliminates dead hair and maintains the coat at a certain texture level.

When dried out, the dog should again be placed on the grooming table for the final touch-up work. This involves intense brushing out, always against the natural growth, scissor work, the evening up of the bracelets, the shaping of the topknot and tail pompom, the correct shaping of the legs, and the like.

Hair in the ears is a problem with all long-coated dogs. The inner ear should be free of hair, and periodic groomings will accomplish this, but only an expert should probe inside the ear. Professionals use tweezers, but the safe rule to follow is to take out of the ear only as much hair as you can with your thumb and forefinger working together. Yank it out quickly, but be careful about going down too deep. If the hair within the ear is damp and waxy, shake a small quantity of antiseptic powder in the ear before pulling, allow it to remain a few minutes, and then proceed. The powder will absorb a great deal of the moisture and make the operation less painful.

In clipping the poodle the general rule is always to clip toward the muzzle, that is, against the natural growth of the hair, except on the back of the forelegs. Clip these downward as the hair runs upward, and when doing the back of the tail clip upward. The clipping of the body against the growth of the hair with a No. 15 or No. 30 blade leaves a short, sleek, and smooth growth. If you do not want the clipping that close, you can operate the clippers toward the tail *with* the growth, using a No. 10 blade. And should that be too close, then you can use a No. 7 blade, either with or against, until you have achieved the desired result.

For the final touch you might spray the dog with pure essential oil of pine diluted in alcohol. This not only leaves a clean and refreshing odor but acts as a repellent to insects.

The matter of giving a puppy its first and second clip is always a worry to most owners, but after the third clip the dog catches on. If you are clipping a puppy for the first time, one way of doing it is for someone to hold the puppy securely in his arms while the operator quickly does the face, feet, and tail. The operation is completed before the puppy realizes it. The other way is to place the puppy on the table—he will have to be held—and without attempting to clip, start the clippers and hold them close to his ears for a few moments to accustom him to the whir of the motor. Turn off and repeat and move the machine around his body. Then, taking a firm hold of the muzzle, proceed despite all objections.

The following directions for types of clip are set up for standards. The rules are the same, however, for miniatures and toys. Bear in mind that the entire clip must be in proportion to the size and conformation of the dog. Some poodles have long legs, others short; some have long necks; others lack a depth of loin. It is no secret that the "tricks of a tailor" have to be employed. A few years' experience will be required before it can be said of you, as Samuel Butler said: "He could distinguish and divide a hair twixt south and southwest side." The poodle Club of America realizes it is impossible to draw up a definite set of rules for clipping all poodles, but as long as you are a poodle lover, it feels positive your first attempt will not prove disappointing if the basic rules are adhered to.

THE ENGLISH SADDLE CLIP

In starting to clip at the muzzle, the important thing is to hold the muzzle firmly with one hand. Any turning of the head may result in unevenness. Start the clipping at a point on the throat approximating the Adam's apple. This will be about three to four inches under the jaw line. Clip to the tip of the lower lip. Now lay back the ears and start the clippers at the top of the ear hole; clip in a straight line to the outside corner of the eye. Next, clip from the same place at the top of the ear hole to a point where you started under the jaw. Then clip away all hair in the area defined, at all times clipping toward the muzzle. Be careful along the lower eyelids. Do not stretch the skin as irritation may result.

In working around the lips, maintain more than firm hold on the muzzle, for an exposed tongue may be cut by the clippers. The eyes and ears follow, and special attention must be paid to them in order to

perfect a true poodle expression. Do not cut the hair over the eyes. At the inside corner of each eye make a slight V in reverse, the depth of the V to be determined by the length of the head. If the head is short the V should be increased, as this will tend to make the head appear longer. Should the head be long, you may not want to make a V; in this case, clip on a straight line between the inside corners of the eyes. Then proceed to the ear again and clip off all hair in front of the ear flap so that it may lie close to the head.

Do the feet next. The dog may sit down. Hold the paw with your thumb on top and press against the pads underneath with your fingers to push the skin up between the toes. Clip the foot up to and just beyond the mark left by the removal of the dew-claws. At least one inch of pastern should be left showing. The line represents the bottom line of the bracelet. If the dog is more on the leggy side, you will want to raise the bracelet. The bracelet should measure about two and three-quarter inches in width, depending of course on the length of leg and the size of dog.

Clip the forearm from the top of the bracelet line upward until the

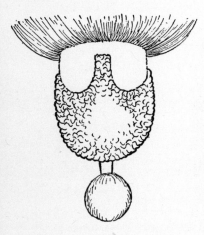

clippers come to an automatic stop against the elbow bone. In doing the back of the forelegs, clip downward as the hair grows upward. The back paws may be done while the dog is sitting with leg extended, or if the dog prefers to stand the leg may be pulled backward or toward you. Clip upward so that at least one inch of pastern is left showing.

The tail should be done next. Clip downward except on the underside; there clip upward, with the hair. About three and a half inches of skin should show on the tail, not including the pompom. The amount of skin to show depends somewhat on the length of the tail. If docked too short, more hair will have to remain on the end. If too long, the hair of the pompom will have to be scissored off at the top to a point where it is practically even with the tip of the tail. Upon completion of the tail, rub on some hand lotion.

The setting of the pattern on the hindquarters calls for a sharp eye and patience. If setting the pattern for the first time, it is recommended that the entire back first be scissored so that about one inch of hair is left. There is no definite rule as to where the saddle should begin. It depends upon the length of the back and what is most pleasing to the eye. Usually the scissoring goes forward to the last rib. After the scissoring, start with the bracelets on the back legs. Put your fingers on the hock joint and start the clippers there, then make a circular space around the entire leg. This space should not be too wide, about an inch or so, and the bottom spacing should be at a slight angle breaking downward toward the front. The second spacing or band comes opposite the stifle, and most people prefer to have this spacing horizontal.

Now for the saddle, and time to make haste slowly. Study the illustration above showing the saddle as it appears from a point directly overhead. When you have determined the point where the ruff is to start, go back an inch or so and clip forward to the beginning of the ruff. Clip this inch or so band around the body down on each side to a point a little higher than the tuck-up. Then make your symmetrical curve by working slowly backward toward the rump. Work slowly in circular cuts and do not attempt to make the curve in one fell swoop. That portion of the curve farthest back should be about seven inches from the set of the tail. To make the curve on the other side of the body, you can put the dog on the floor and get a bird's-eye look at him, or stand him on the table and operate from high altitude. A piece of string might be used to measure the corresponding points of the curve.

For the final brush out, the dog should lie on his side and the

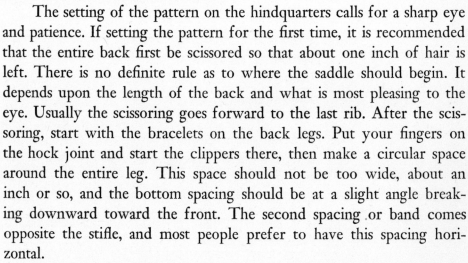

brushing commence at a point nearest the saddle. He should be brushed out bit by bit, brushing toward the feet. If any mats remain they must be eliminated; pull them apart with the fingers and then brush out. The brushing will finish up at the head. Then start all over again at the head and brush toward the muzzle. This brushing against the natural growth, which must be repeated, makes for harshness of coat.

You will then level off by scissoring. Naturalness is the object. Follow the lines of the body. If the dog is long, you will want to scissor the hair on the upper portion of the brisket somewhat shorter than standard, and to shorten the hair on the back of the thigh and under the tail. If the legs are short, the underside of the ruff should be scissored so as to make the dog look taller. How bracelets may be lowered on a dog with short legs or raised if a dog is too leggy has already been discussed. In scissoring the bracelets, comb down and trim along the line left by the clipper, then comb upward and trim along the clipper line on the upper portion of the bracelet. Then the entire bracelet can be properly shaped. The scissoring should leave an effect of smoothness and evenness.

The pack should be trimmed along the line left by the clipping, and then the pack should be gone over lightly with the scissors, cutting off all unevenness found in the hair that does not curl up. In order to insure a tight pack, spray or sprinkle a little warm water on the pack and then pat it down or cover it as tightly as possible with a towel.

The finishing touch is fastening back the hair from the eyes with a barrette or ribbon.

THE CONTINENTAL CLIP

The Continental is identical with the English Saddle from the beginning of the ruff to the tip of the muzzle. The only difference, as will be observed in the illustration, is in the hindquarters. The face, feet, and tail are done in precisely the same manner, but the coat on the hindquarters is clipped entirely clean save for the pompoms on the hips and the bracelets covering the hock joints.

The bracelets on the hock joints may be horizontal or they may have a slant downward to the front. They should be shaped in accordance with the illustration.

The best results in this clip are secured by using a No. 15 blade, clipping against the natural growth. The clipping should be done two days before the show.

The pompoms on the hips are optional. If the hip bones show, however, you certainly should cover them with pompoms. These should

be from two to three inches in diameter, depending again on the size of the dog. In order to place them properly, center the top of a can or some other household item of proper diameter on the hip bone. Clip a perfect circle around it, and in finishing off, scissor them so that they have a convex surface, similar in shape to the yolk of a fried egg.

THE PUPPY CLIP

The Puppy Clip involves clipping only the face, feet, and tail while the rest of the coat remains long. There is no rule or requirement as to how long the coat should be, but it should be at least three inches in length. Lately there has been tendency to clip it shorter than three inches.

The puppy should be brushed out completely as described before,

and the top of the coat should be scissored so that the puppy will look his best in accordance with the natural lines of his body.

Poodles may be exhibited clipped in this style provided they are under one year of age.

THE KENNEL CLIP

The Kennel Clip, as will be noted from the illustration, is similar to the Puppy Clip except that in this style the coat, including the legs, is scissored down so that only an inch or less of coat remains. This type of clip, which requires little coat care, is used when the dog is going to remain in the kennel for some time, and thus derives its name. The coat can be allowed to curl up or can be maintained in a brushed-out condition.

Sometimes a puppy around six months of age does not appear to be gathering a good coat. If so, it is recommended the puppy be so clipped in order to facilitate the growth of the mature hair which is coming in at about this age.

In England this clip is known as the Lamb Trim.

THE ASTRAKHAN CLIP

This clip, though somewhat popular in England, is not used to any great extent in the United States. It has considerable merit as a utility type of clip. In this style the clipping machine is not used at any point. Only the scissors are employed. The coat is scissored down over the entire body, leaving about one-half inch or less of hair, which curls up and gives the coat an appearance similar to that of the Astrakhan lamb. The face is scissored and so is the tail. The feet are done in terrier fashion. The hair on the ears may be left long or scissored down to the same length as the body coat.

THE SPORTING CLIP

This is an all-purpose clip suitable for both town and country and is becoming more popular every day. Adaptable to the standard or the miniature, it allows for a display of the beautiful lines of the body and yet is practical in that very little brushing is involved except on the

legs. It is liked by those who desire a fashionable-looking poodle but without too sleeky an appearance.

Do the face and tail first with a No. 15 blade. A mustache is allowable if desired. In doing the body you have your choice of a No. 7 or No. 10 blade, depending upon how close you want the body clipped. Start the blade at the back of the neck, in the center, and clip on a straight line back to the beginning of the tail. Then continue clipping in the same manner, widening the path until you reach a point between the shoulders and the upper arm on the front portion of the dog, and on the hind legs, a point on the loin or upper thigh. No observable line of demarkation should be left separating the body clip from the hair on the legs. Work downward with a No. 7 blade for about two inches all along the horizontal line usually left in the Dutch cut. This will smooth off the dog. The front portion of the dog should be clipped clean down the brisket to the beginning of the chest, leaving, however, some growth of hair on the chest. The topknot should then be scissored to the right shape, and then the legs. The legs may be left full as shown in the illustration, or scissored down even thinner—thinner in the summertime at least. In using the scissors in this clip and in the clips to follow, work the scissors toward the legs, or down. If you cut in a horizontal manner, ridges will be left in the coat.

THE NON-SPORTING CLIP

This represents a fairly new fashion quite cosmopolitan in character. It is primarily for miniatures but looks well on standards who are not too bulky.

The clipping is done in precisely the same manner as the Sporting Clip except that a small circular mustache and beard are left on the face, and the feet are not clipped but scissored so as to leave terrier feet. The hair within the pads of the feet should, however, be cleaned out. The hair on the ears is clipped inside and out with a No. 10 blade in order to give a clean-shaven effect, and, as stated previously, the edges of the ears may be smoothed by using a No. 30 blade.

It is advisable to clip the brisket fairly clean to provide for some space showing between the legs, which are scissored shorter than in the Sporting Clip but left longer than the Kennel Clip. Examine the legs well before scissoring. They may be slightly bowed, in which event straighten out by tailoring.

THE DUTCH-CUT CLIP

Among non-exhibitors this is by far the most popular style of clip, and most miniatures and toys are so stylized. It does not look any too well on large standards.

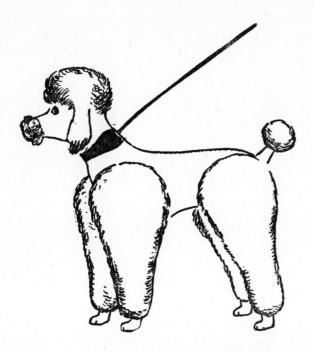

It is most difficult to lay down any set of rules for undertaking this clip because each owner wants his dog done in a particular style. Some want a high topknot; others want large and puffy pantaloons. The variations are many, even to the extent that the tassels on the ears should be done in just a certain way and no other.

Do the feet and tail first with a No. 15 blade: then the face, leaving room for a mustache and beard to be shaped later by scissoring to the style preferred; some like just the mustache, and clip the chin bare. Again, depending on how close you want the dog clipped, you can use a No. 15 blade and clip from the tail to the neck, or a No. 10 blade and clip with the growth of the hair from the neck to the tail. Usually, on the average miniature, the width of the clipper determines the space between the lines where the pantaloons start on the rump. On the withers the space is slightly wider because the body is wider at this point. Then go to the front of the dog, and, holding his muzzle firmly in your left hand, tilt his head up slightly and clean off the front of the neck by clipping downward. Only the person clipping will be able to determine just how far down the clipping should extend. If the dog has a long neck do not go down too far.

Then clip down the neck on one side and establish your pattern for the front pantaloons. If the dog is short-legged you will want the pantaloons well up on the shoulders; if long-legged, just the opposite. Establish the pattern on one leg, bringing it down the ribs to the belly. Use short cuts in this shaping. The top portions of the pantaloons in this clip are much larger than in the Royal Dutch, that is, they cover a larger area. But again, it depends on conformation. If the dog has a long body you will want the front pantaloons brought farther to the back.

Next, proceed to the other side of the dog and make the same pattern. Then make your pattern on the rump for the rear pantaloons. The ears should be done inside and out with a No. 10 blade, and tassels may be left on the ears or the ears clipped bare.

Finish off by scissoring off the topknot, mustache and beard, tail pompom and the pantaloons, the latter to be of any size. In most instances a slight tapering effect so that the pantaloons are smaller around the feet gives the most pleasing effect.

THE ROYAL DUTCH CLIP

This clip is practically indentical with the regular Dutch Cut except that the front pantaloons do not cover as wide an area but are placed up higher on the shoulders so as to provide a "high pockets" effect.

The clip is usually found on large miniatures or small standards.

Many prefer the lower portion of the legs scissored much thinner than shown in the illustration, and tapered down toward the feet.

In this clip the topknot can be either regular style, that is,

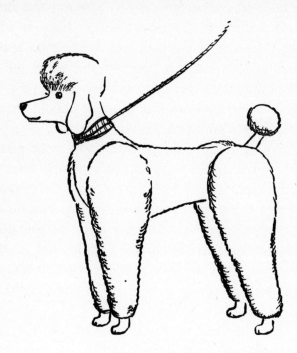

rounded, or in Dutchman's Hat fashion, which is somewhat flat.

Another feature of this clip is that the pantaloons may be round or scissored on the outside so as to give a square, boxy appearance.

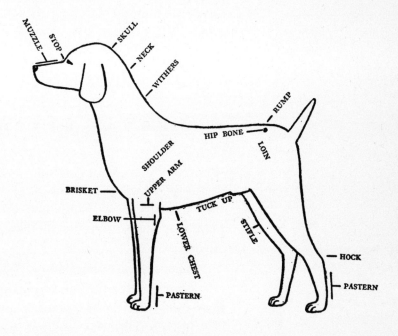

chapter 6

BREEDING

Ancestors of ancestors are reckoned.

LATIN PROVERB

OF ALL THE SWEET MYSTERIES OF LIFE, BREEDING IS WITH-out doubt the most perplexing and aggravating, yet it is fascinating in its challenge. For hundreds of years inquisitive students, naturalists, and scientists have spent an incredible amount of time in library, laboratory, and farm, probing the secrets of heredity so that types and characteristics might be improved. This research has produced a vast amount of knowledge which has been successfully utilized in the breeding of better livestock and poultry, and the raising of superior types of corn, wheat, and other vegetation. But it cannot be said that any pronounced advance has been made in the breeding of dogs. The knowledge available has not been fully used. Breeding, like marriage, should not be entered into lightly. Successful breeding demands intelligence, which means the practical application of the scientific knowledge we have.

Because poodles have become popular and increased in number, we are bound to find many below-average specimens. But established kennels possess the necessary know-how and are painstaking in their breeding programs. They devote thought to each situation and know what they are doing, as opposed to the careless and indiscriminate breeder, who places intuition above intellect.

The somewhat serious situation that exists today has two causes: First there is the quantitative breeder, he who breeds in such volume that there is automatically imputed to him the reputation of an authority, by virtue of an incorrect inference that the more he breeds the more he knows about breeding. The other specter is the individual who, upon detecting the slightest manifestation of libido in his poodle, whether real or pretended, desires an immediate mating regardless of color, blood lines, or possible results. Often he mistakenly believes that a mating will most certainly result in a perfect counterpart of his beloved.

Although the perfect poodle has not yet been whelped, and probably never will be, we can try. Nothing exists that cannot be improved upon. Good conscience forces us to admit that some of the specimens of today are poor when judged against the ideal poodle. For example, in many standards the skull is not sufficiently full, the eyes are too close together, the muzzle is undesirably pointed, the feet are flat, and the toes spread. In many miniatures the body is too long, the legs short, and the ears set too high with insufficient leather. And in some toys we find round popeyes and high-flying ears. These deficiencies may be corrected if there is some thoughtful adherence to the elementary principles of heredity.

The life of the average poodle owner is far too short for any comprehensive understanding of the complexities of genetics, which involves recessive telophase, heterosis, epigenisis, zygotes, and allelemorphs. And if these are not sufficient for a Cole Porter verse we have additional terrifying nomenclature, such as discordant, delayed, modified, and non-fluctuating dominances, interspecific hybridization, triploidy, and, of all things, secondary spermatocytes and autoteraploids.

There is a breeding problem attached to each breed: Great Danes have a deafness factor, collies have an eye situation which must always be guarded against, and other breeds have spotting factors. With the poodle, color seems to be the commanding problem, for although the rule requires solidity of color, of late there has been an alarming tendency to disregard it. This departure from the path of rectitude can be attributed to a lack of knowledge regarding color breeding, although in some instances it is deliberately planned for purposes of amusement. We have too many mismarked poodles for whom there is no excuse, and too many of differing shade and hue. The names platinum, café au lait, and the like sound glamorous enough but are meaningless unless there is stability, a solidity of color—without shadings or gradations. Solidity of color cannot be attained unless there is purity of color. The laws of heredity teach us how to secure and perpetuate pure colors.

Black is the dominant color and prevails over all others. White and brown are recessive. These three are the foundation colors. As a result of intercolor breeding we have blue, gray, grizzle, platinum, old pewter, and silver, and we have cream, apricot, champagne, chestnut, parchment, mauve, café au lait, and cinnamon. It is sometimes quite obvious that such fanciful names, often applied arbitrarily, are not truly descriptive; they may be names but do not represent pure color. With poodles, colors are organic, therefore susceptible to exact description. Our colors should not be treated in terms of chromatic tones or classified according to the jargon of fashion writers. Color is controlled by genes, and the dilutions—that is, the blues, silvers, etc. —are the result of additional modifying factors.

Efficient breeding requires an understanding of the cell, the chromosomes, the genes, and what is dominant and recessive. The beginning of life is a cell; it is an entity and represents the unit of every living organism. Your poodle is composed of hundreds of thousands of cells more or less uniform in shape and size. There are two types of cells, body cells and germ or sex cells. Each cell contains a fixed number of chromosomes. These are tiny bead-like units within the cell. Each species has a different number of chromosomes although, as stated above, within each species the number is fixed. In man, each cell contains forty-eight chromosomes. The cell of a mosquito contains six, and in corn there are twenty. Unfortunately, it is not known how many chromosomes there are in the cell of a dog, but for purposes of discussion we will assume there are forty. Chromosomes always travel in pairs, so when we speak of forty chromosomes we mean twenty pairs. If you could but examine one body cell of your poodle you would see these forty chromosomes and observe that although each one appears to be separate and somewhat different in size, yet there are two in each cell that are a pair because although not entirely so, they are practically indentical in shape and appearance and operate together like two cops on a beat.

Within the chromosomes are found the well-advertised genes. Genes are called units, determiners, or factors. The last term is most acceptable, because they impart the factor they carry, whether it is for color, expression, ears, eyes, feet, coat—yes, even personality; and speaking of coat, the genes even affect quality and character of texture. In short, the genes are responsible for all and everything, with the possible exception of a few minor traits known to be acquired with training. As we shall see shortly, every puppy has a different set of genes, and that is why no two dogs can ever be identical. Genes, therefore, may be likened to human fingerprints, no two sets of which are identical.

Let us examine your poodle puppy. He is represented by an accumulation of body cells each of which contains twenty pairs of chromosomes. He received ten pairs from the germ cell of his dam and ten pairs from the germ cell of his sire. His body grows by cell division, and in this process, each member of each pair of chromosomes divides. This leaves four members of each pair, two of each of these members go into one new body cell and two members of each pair go into another new body cell, therefore each new cell possesses the exact number of pairs of chromosomes as the original or parent cell. Furthermore, each cell contains identical genes.

As the puppy grows, his germ cells form in his reproductive glands. The germ cells also multiply by division but the mechanics are quite different. Each member of each pair of chromosomes does not divide, but one member of a pair goes into one sex cell and the other member goes into another sex cell. In order to play the game, it is suggested that you lay out on the table before you twenty pairs of buttons representing the chromosomes within the body cell. Each pair of buttons is of course to be different. Now separate these buttons into two columns, each column to have one of each pair. The column on the left represents the chromosomes received from the dam and the column on the right represents the chromosomes received from the sire. A germ cell is to be created, and nature has issued a mandate to the effect that the germ cell is to contain only one-half the number of chromosomes found in the body cell, in our case, twenty chromosomes. This is for the simple reason that later on in life, when breeding takes place, this germ cell will unite with its mate, which also has only twenty chromosomes, and the forty chromosomes will be restored. Getting back to the beginning of the germ cell we are to create, we pick up from the table our twenty pairs of buttons and shake them together, in our hand. The germ cell is to contain one-half of the buttons (chromosomes), but not any old half—one of each pair; so you pick out from the forty mixed buttons one of each pair. These twenty go into the germ cell which is now created. Can you determine at this point just which of the buttons came from the left-hand column, the dam, or which came from the right-hand column, the sire? Of course not. One germ cell may get fourteen chromosomes from the dam and six from the sire. It would be possible for a germ cell to contain nineteen chromosomes from the dam and only one from the sire. The only proviso is that each germ cell receive one-half of each pair. Other germ cells are formed, each having one chromosome of each pair, yet it can never be known just how many came from the sire and how many from the dam. This process by which the chromosomes are halved in the germ cells is termed reduction.

As our puppy reaches maturity he is bred. Of his thousands of germ cells, each contains a set of chromosomes. It is usually stated that the germ cell contains all the heredity factors. What is meant is that the germ cell is the carrier and transmitter of the chromosomes which contain the genes. When the spermatazoon, the cell of the male, reaches and fertilizes the nucleus of the ova cell of the female, what is to be the living organism is created. The two germ cells, each containing twenty chromosomes, unite, the two members of each pair come together, forming the same number of pairs of chromosomes found in the body cell, in this case twenty pairs, one-half from each parent. It has been said that in every union there is a mystery—a certain invisible bond which must not be disturbed. Although the germ cells contain the same number of chromosomes, the genes in every pair of chromosomes are rarely identical, and that is why every puppy is different—because of a different set of genes. Nature never seeks to maintain the status quo but varies things a bit, at the same time always striving to express the dominant.

This explanation emphasizes the importance of line and inbreeding. Although many deny any validity to the "grandparent theory," it is manifest that puppies, as well as people, sometimes closely resemble their grandparents. Why wouldn't they when most of the genes in the germ cells involved in creating them came from the resembled grandparent and therefore were the preponderant factors transmitted? It should be observed by now that the matter of breeding is not unlike a game of chance, as it all depends upon the set of genes within the chromosomes.

Color is obviously an inherited factor, but it is the control of color that is important. In other words, how do you make the genes work for you? By dominant we do not necessarily mean an overpower-

"Which twin has the Toni?"
Lithograph by Gladys Emerson Cook

Gerald H. Green,
courtesy of American Magazine

Reprinted from March 1950 Esquire.
Copyright 1950 by Esquire, Inc.

Mr. Bambino, Ha'penny, and Miss Penelope, owned by Arthur Whitney and Franklin Hughes, New York

HERO WORSHIP

Copyright, 1950, New York Herald Tribune Inc.

"The Unseen Audience" by H. T. Webster

Reprinted by permission of the New York Herald Tribune, Inc.

"He's not much good but he gives the other dogs a laugh."

Courtesy of Carl Rose and Collier's

"You and your cute ideas! Nobody has looked at us all day."

photos by Marthe Krueger

Michette, owned by
Mrs. Frederick C. Shorey

Bubbles, C. D., C. D. X.,
and U. D. Black miniature
owned by Ethel S. Nathan-
son, New York. Bubbles
starred in the movie short,
School for Dogs. He has an
up-and-coming son named
Soda Pop.

photo by Hanks

"The Bride and Groom," modern ceramic by Jane Callender

photo by Farr

Modern ceramic

Courtesy Lilliput Magazine, *London*

ing color or trait to which everything else is subordinate. It merely means possession of the upper hand, the ability to override the recessive. And recessive does not automatically mean something bad or undesirable; it means that it is concealed, whereas the dominant is always visible. With black the dominant color, any other color factor that remains in hiding and is not visible is termed recessive. Color is dependent upon several gene pairs. If two members of a pair of factors are alike in all respects, it is said that the poodle is homozygous. That is to say, if two members of a pair of genes are alike with respect to black (or white or brown) the poodle is homozygous as to color. Such a poodle may be called a pure black. Even though the pedigree shows all black ancestors, one can never be certain whether the poodle is pure for color, and this happens to be just the one thing poodle breeders want to know.

When two members of a pair of genes are in contrast for color or another factor, the poodle is called heterozygous. To be homozygous the puppy must inherit the gene for black from both parents. If the pair inherited is not precisely alike the dog is heterozygous. This dog is called a hybrid, but there is no sinister implication to the word. It merely means that he received only one gene for his outward appearance color or trait. The gene for the other color or trait is not expressed and remains concealed within him.

Let us breed a pure black to a white and assume that there are no mismarking factors involved. The litter is eight puppies. All of these puppies will be black, that is black in appearance. They have received one white gene from their mother and one black gene from, in this case, the father, but the white gene, white being recessive, is covered up by the black gene. All of these puppies would be known as hybrid for color. Now let us see what Mendel did. He worked with flowers, but he could just as well have worked with poodles. If he took two of these puppies and bred them together and if there were eight in the resulting litter, he would have found that this second generation litter would contain two pure blacks, four hybrid blacks, and two pure whites. If he bred another pair in the first generation litter and if there were four in the litter, one would be pure black, two would be hybrid black, and one would be pure white. In other words, turning to the illustration, if any two of the hybrid blacks of the first generation were bred together, or if one of them was bred to another similar hybrid even from another litter, the expected ratio would be, out of every four puppies: one pure black, which received two black genes

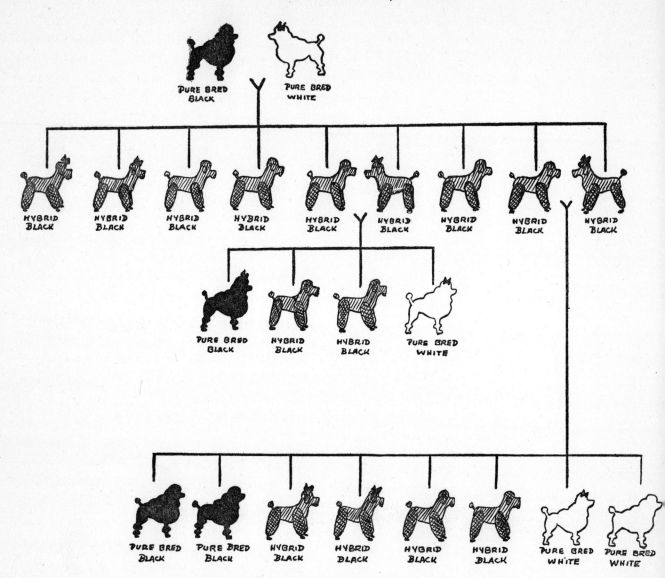

Diagram illustrating the 1:2:1 expected color ratio when two similar hybrids are bred

from each parent, two hybrid blacks, and one pure white, which received an identical pair of white genes from each parent. This is the law of segregation—how the genes for color (or for any other character) assort themselves from one generation to the next.

The pure blacks in the second generation will breed true, as will the pure whites. Naturally, if you breed two hybrids of the second generation together, they will breed precisely like their parents. One of the leading kennels in the East established its pure white line by using the above procedure. The dam was white as far back as could be traced and the sire was black with a fairly solid black background. The litter was black, with some of the puppies mismarked with white. The entire litter was retained, and those with the blackest pigment inbred for two generations until it was definitely known which were homozygous for white color. When these whites were established, they could not possibly transmit black, as the dominant color was lost. The gene for recessive white could not possibly hide the dominant gene for black.

So, the safest rule to follow is to breed solid color to solid color. Brown and white being recessive, we know that such color characteristics require two genes to produce that color effect, one gene being contributed by each parent. In other words, the recessive color, desirable in this case, must come from both sides of the family.

I have frequently been asked what color puppies will result from a proposed mating where different colors are involved. It is difficult to say. We have not yet reached the point where we insist that pedigrees contain a notation as to the color of the ancestors, and in most cases such information would not necessarily be conclusive. We would have to know the color of the litter out of which the bride and groom came, and then we would have to look into the color characteristics of the bride's dam and sire as well as the groom's, and then find out the color results of each of the four parents when bred to other colors—an almost impossible task. Also, the genes contain factors other than the color factor. There is what is called the dilution factor, which turns a black to a blue or even to silver. This factor is independent of the genes for color, and it may or may not be possessed by a particular pair of dogs.

What is true of color inheritance is precisely the same for eyes, ears, feet, skull, or any other trait or characteristic. If you breed two toys with high-flying ears the litter will have high-flying ears. And if you breed two miniatures with long caterpillar backs you cannot expect a litter with compactness of body. As shyness is inherited, the breeding of two shys will necessarily result in offspring not to be noted for aggressiveness. Should you breed a dog with an undesirable recessive characteristic, either visible or hidden, even to the champion of champions, you are still taking a chance.

Edna M. Dubuis of the Jackson Laboratory stated it in *The New England Dog* for May 1948: "Recessive characteristics require two genes to produce their effect in an individual, one gene being contributed by each of the parents. A recessive characteristic which is seen is, therefore, always purebred and must come from both sides of the family. One recessive gene may be carried by an individual, but when it is carried in a hybrid state it is always covered up or hidden in the individual by the corresponding dominant gene. Thus, recessive characteristics may appear to skip one or many generations, as they are not seen. This is in contrast to dominant characteristics, which do not skip a generation and which are always seen.

"As the individual does not always show the characteristic, it is often difficult for the breeder to ascertain whether or not the recessive is there. By mating animals which carry recessive traits to animals which are purebred for the corresponding dominant traits, it is possible to keep the recessives covered up for twenty or fifty generations or more. It is only when an animal which carries one gene for a recessive trait meets a like partner, who also carries one gene for the same characteristic, that the two recessive genes are allowed to come together (one from each parent) and produce their effect in some of the offspring."

We have seen how, in order to secure a line which is pure and therefore solid, it is usually necessary to do some inbreeding. This is the breeding of closely related individuals, such as brother to sister, father to daughter, mother to son, and sometimes first cousin to first cousin. Despite a seeming aversion to inbreeding, it is not undesirable and it should be indulged in to a far greater extent than it is at present. Much of this feeling comes from those who have read that continued inbreeding of guinea pigs led to the conclusion that inbreeding is deleterious and results in loss of vigor. This is true when generation after generation is inbred, but this, of course, is not being advocated. Others dislike inbreeding because it unites and intensifies the bad characteristics as well as the good, but certainly we are not going to inbreed when the bad characteristics outweigh the good, or whenever there are any outstanding serious faults either present or possible. It is only by inbreeding that we may secure identical genes in each pair of chromosomes.

Laurence H. Snyder, in *The Principles of Heredity,* plainly points out: "The facts are that inbreeding does not create any weaknesses or defects. In itself it is not harmful. What inbreeding does is to increase rapidly the homozygosity of the population, to isolate any pure lines, to bring to light in the homozygous condition any recessive factors which may have been carried in the heterozygous state in the stock. We have seen that most mutations are recessives, and that most are harmful. It follows that, because of natural selection, the individuals having the harmful genes in the homozygous state will be eliminated. This leaves, however, many individuals in the population carrying one or more of these recessive deleterious genes in the heterozygous state. Under a system of random mating, these are to a large extent carried along, in the heterozygous condition, from generation to generation. Under any system of inbreeding, however, the heterozygotes in the population rapidly become less frequent and the homozygotes more frequent. Under these conditions all the hidden recessive genes become expressed in homozygous form. Many of these affect vigor, fertility, and viability. Thus the race as a whole tends to degenerate under inbreeding.

"Not only are deleterious characters brought to light, however, but other genetic characters of the race become apparent through increasing homozygosity. Some of these characters may be beneficial, or at least not harmful. Thus, if rigid selection accompanies inbreeding, it is usually possible to preserve certain of the desirable combinations in more or less homozygous form. Large numbers of individuals must usually be discarded in the process, however. Moderate inbreeding, with careful selection, has been the basis of the building up and improving of most of the modern breeds and varieties of livestock and cultivated plants.

"In any group of individuals with which man is concerned, it is desirable to know what hereditary traits are carried. Inbreeding quickly tells this by bringing to light all hidden recessives. Pure lines are rapidly formed, and from these the desired ones may be selected and the rest discarded. Pure lines are of considerable value in many ways. They may be, because of selection, free from defects, particularly hidden defects. They will breed true for all their characters."

The terms "particolor" and "mismarking" are frequently used interchangeably, but there is a great difference which is important to breeders. Particolor means a dog of two distinct colors, whereas mismarking consists of white spots, usually found on the chin, throat, chest, feet, and tail of blacks or browns, or brown spots on blacks, or black spots on whites. The intelligent breeder should never produce particolor or mismarked animals unless experimenting to discover the homozygous; if they are produced they should never be sold, since they undoubtedly carry the ability to transmit mismarking. They represent pollution. Many breeders, if they sell or give away a particolor, do so with the understanding that no signed application for registration goes with the puppy. This is an effective control method, as breeding in the future is unlikely if the dog is not registered. Particolors are as undesirable as they were years ago. As early as 1879 one was exhibited in Brighton, and Joyce, who was present, observed: "His peculiar markings apparently did not find favor with the judges."

Particolors are the result of unforgivable breeding that gives no consideration to color background. It is to be hoped that pedigree notations of the color of four generations of ancestors will assist the amateur breeder in this respect. If particolors are bred, the utmost confusion will certainly result should any of the litter be bred later. Parti bred to parti will breed true—the entire litter will be particolored. If you breed a parti to a solid (not necessarily a pure color), the result will be a litter all of which, regardless of color and markings, have the factor and ability to transmit mismarking—although some of the litter will be solid color and some will be mismarked.

If you breed two solid-colored poodles who carry the mismarking factor, the result will be, out of four, one definitely mismarked, one solid, and two which carry the mismarking ability. Here are the rules as stated by Dr. C. C. Little of the Jackson Laboratory:

1. Do not use a mismarked dog for breeding, regardless of any good points it may possess, unless you want and expect mismarked puppies.
2. Whenever a given mating between two solid-colored parents produce a mismarked puppy, remember:
   a. It will probably do so again.
   b. Approximately two-thirds of the puppies which show no white markings carry (hidden) the ability to produce mismarked offspring when mated to other solid-colored dogs which have the same hidden ability.
   c. The same two-thirds will transmit to their descendants the ability to produce mismarked offspring.
3. When a sire or dam throws mismarked puppies, they will transmit the ability to do so to at least one-half of their progeny, no matter what mate is used and no matter whether the progeny is itself solid-colored.

How does this work out in actual practice? A few years ago two leading kennels carefully planned a scientific mating. The result justified the forethought, as out of the litter came one of the finest poodles ever bred in the United States. The sire was white from a long line of established white champions, and the dam was black with an equally good background of champions of solid color. The litter of nine was black, but three of the puppies had white mismarkings. Where did these mismarks come from? Somewhere, not too far back in the pedigree, one of the ancestors received and retained the ability to transmit mismarking. These mismarked puppies were put to sleep on their everlasting couch to prevent their transmitting such mismarking or the ability to do so. That left six puppies, solid black, but later one of these puppies was bred to a black bitch whose ancestry was substantially solid black. The result was nine puppies, all of which were black but one had a tiny white mismark on his throat. This bears out the rule expressed by Dr. Little, but it is quite probable the ratio of two-thirds decreases as solid is bred to solid.

Since the importance of solid color is emphasized, you may ask why breeders continue to breed blacks to browns, browns to whites, and apricots to browns, when it is not too difficult to secure the homozygous type. The reason is that breeders who have purity of color established in their kennels will frequently breed to other colors for other factors, such as better coat, eyes, and ears, expression, or even personality. But this calls for knowledge and experience and should be undertaken only by professionals. The breeding of two hybrids is frequently most advisable as each will supply some dominant trait lacking in the other.

Line breeding is also desirable. This involves the breeding of those not too closely related, such as grandfather to granddaughter, grandmother to grandson, uncles to nieces, and aunts to nephews. It is generally accepted as the safest method if it is feared that a bad trait or traits will come to the front as a result of inbreeding.

Outcrossing is a term applied to the mating of two who have no common ancestry. This method cannot be relied on; it is a gamble, but it is sometimes used by expert breeders.

Backcrossing is the breeding of a pure for the recessive color, to a black that is suspected of not being pure black but a hybrid: the breeding, for example, of a pure brown or pure white to a black to determine if that black carries the recessive gene for the other color. If you use a brown for this purpose and if, in a litter of not less than five, one of the puppies is brown, it received the gene for brown from both parents and it is known that the black is hybrid and not pure.

In discussing breeding, one constantly hears the terms type and selection. By type we mean all that the poodle is, inside or out, his color, coat, head, chest, general conformation, character, personality, and expression. Type is le tout ensemble—the whole considered in its entirety. The best type is naturally that which most closely resembles the ideal poodle, or which represents the very best in the combined influences of all the favorable genes. Selection simply means discrimination: Be intelligent in your selection of a mate, after careful study has indicated what you hope to accomplish. Selection, however, should mean something more to the poodle owner; it should signify sticking to the proven and established blood lines that year after year have produced the finest poodles.

Speaking of selection, Miss Louise Branch of the Carillon Kennels, says: "Every kennel carries in mind the ultimate goal and sets up a breeding program designed to lead to and sustain its ideal of the perfect poodle. The individual breeder should have definitely fixed in his mind what he hopes to achieve and exercise abundant intelligence in selecting a mate.

"We are taking one factor at a time and developing this characteristic by judicious selection which at the same time implies the breeding out of undesirable factors.

"We are attempting to establish a strain of black standards having complete purity of color without losing any of the other desirable characteristics, and emphasis is being placed upon temperament and personality. Our goal is a keen, alert, responsive dog of high intelligence and naturally affectionate; one light and graceful in action and structurally sound, thus having the stamina necessary to carry on whatever work is required. The production of a line of blacks noted for purity of color is not so simple as one might think, even though working with a dominant factor. We have seen far too many blacks with overtones of brown or a slate cast to their coat. This is the necessary but unfortunate result of mixing colors in the past. The color of coat, density, and texture are factors that lie deep within the poodle's ancestry. Personality also must be developed through thoughtful breeding, as this factor is inherited, yet it must be cultivated by the ultimate owner of the puppy. General indifference, shyness, and ill manners frequently give the impression of a negative personality probably coupled with a bad disposition, and this is very likely due to faulty breeding."

Which is the more important, the sire or the dam? You frequently hear breeders predicting all the good things to come provided the sire "will assert himself vigorously." All things being equal, and it taking two to make a bargain, the dam is more important if only from a standpoint of nutrition, and many are the cases wherein the dam controls—no matter to whom she is bred; she produces a great uniformity of type. Furthermore, we have seen how the production of puppies of excellent substance and quality is dependent upon the combination of genes originated in the grandparents, though transmitted by sire and dam.

The best sire is one termed "proven"; that is, his ability to transmit at least a majority of his best characteristics—those inherited from his parents—is established. We have had champions from nondescript parents and we have had many superb champion sires who never came close to producing an excellent specimen regardless of to whom bred. We now know why that is, because when the germ cells in the sire were formed with one-half the number of chromosomes, their cells received a majority of chromosomes from one poor parent. If I were breeding my dog today I think I would choose the best sire in the United States and breed to that sire's sire.

There are a few people who belittle the practice of securing stud service from the finest of champions, but there is no better method known. If a champion at stud possesses all desirable characteristics and is the type of your dog, if his progeny has been good and his ancestors had the same visible characteristics, then your chance of getting better than average puppies is greater than if you bred to an unknown. If the sire does not possess what you want, do not use him because he cannot transmit what he does not have—he cannot hand down any excellent trait unless he has it. Obviously the same goes for the dam.

Whatever type of breeding is employed, size should be bred to size. Do not think that by breeding a small sire to a large dam, or vice versa, the puppies will be of mean size. There will be no equalization, and the chances are some will be small and some large. And do not be too hasty about breeding. Generally speaking, the sire may be bred at about a year and a half, and the dam not until two years.

So much is known—but there is much more that we have to know. Despite the untiring efforts of breeders to eliminate the light amber color in the eyes of browns, it still persists in many strains, and the breeding of browns to blacks who have dark eyes has not resulted in any permanent change. Eye color is due to pigment in the iris cells. A light eye has more branched pigment cells than a dark eye. The brown, having liver pigment, completely lacks black pigment. The only possible suggestion that can be made is to select a dark-eyed mate. Dark eyes are dominant over light. Also, the inbreeding of browns with dark eyes would do much toward overcoming this problem.

The matter of pigmentation requires further study and effort. It evidently has no influences on coat color, and we have seen the darkest of browns with light amber eyes. Insofar as pigmentation is concerned, to the geneticist all dogs are either black or liver. A great deal depends upon what genes are present in the formation of the embryo, for when pigmentation commences within the embryo it proceeds to a color point known as liver. If it stops at this point your whites and browns will have liver noses, lips, and eyelids. A true brown will of course have all liver pigmentation. If the pigment formation does not stop at the liver point, it continues on and becomes black.

Another matter of interest is the factor that causes a coat to lighten. Many silvers and grays are born black and only gradually lighten in color. It is usually months before the true color is set. Why it requires so long a time for the dilution factor to settle down and impart the true color is not as yet known. We have noted also that the browns fade out into the light glamour shades previously described. It has been surmised that this is because the color, being recessive, tends to fade out and disappear. But red is also recessive with a cocker spaniel, and blue recessive with a chow-chow, yet these colors do not lighten. With the poodle the best guess is that the lightening process is due to the dilution factor. We have also observed in the care of browns that the color fades out even in the absence of the dilution factor when the dog is exposed to an excessive amount of sunlight or spends a great deal of his time in the salt water. The fading out in this instance is undoubtedly due to the glandular make-up of the hair. A mystery as yet unsolved is where with recessive colors there is a sudden and inexplicable appearance of the dominant. It is mostly found in grays; after a loss of hair because of eczema or other skin irritation, the new growth comes in black.

No individual breeder, however productive, can hope to acquire such knowledge and maintain such records as to formulate the general rules so much needed to guide everyone. Scientific breeding requires the filing and studying of statistics from as many sources as possible. All information relating to the inheritance of factors should be supplied to a central depository. There is such a place at the Jackson Laboratory, Bar Harbor, Maine, where a large-scale scientific study of dogs is being conducted. All who breed poodles are urgently requested to cooperate with this much-needed program by writing the laboratory and requesting forms on which to record and submit information.

A proper environment is absolutely essential for the complete development of any poodle despite his possession of the finest selection of genes. And speaking of environment, would it not be advisable for some to breed for the purpose of returning the poodle to his natural heritage, the water? Lee Smits thinks so. He says: "There is a poodle potential that somebody someday will release. It was as a gun dog, the sportsman's partner, that the breed was developed. We can imagine some French nobleman, after a good day afield, reluctant to shut his poodle in the kennel for the night. Indoors, beside the fire, the Frenchman's poodle entered upon the sophisticated life to which he has now become so perfectly adjusted. He became the favorite of ladies. He was bred more and more for wit and beauty, less and less for hardihood and nose and sporting spirit.

"But those qualities have survived in the modern poodle. In a studio apartment he dreams of field and fen and of game brought to bed through his expert aid.

"Many poodle owners have undoubtedly discovered the sporting spirit in their dogs. For one thing, most poodles are natural retrievers. It only remains for some imaginative breeder to bring to the fore, by scientific selection, the ancient poodle heritage, and then put down poodle entries in field trials to show the world that this handsome patrician is no mere dilettante."

The period of heat in the bitch lasts approximately twenty days and the breeding is usually done between the ninth and eleventh days. She should be wormed about two weeks before the mating; if this has been neglected, she should be wormed two weeks after. As nutrition is most vital at this point, she should be fed nourishing food with plenty of meat and a teaspoon of Vitamin E once a day. She should lead her regularly established life and receive the same amount of exercise to which she has been accustomed.

The puppies are due to arrive sixty-three days after the breeding, but the whelping might be a few days before or a few days later. You will find, however, that poodles usually maintain regularity in their delivery schedule. If you do not intend exhibiting the dog, she should be closely clipped a few days before whelping time, with the belly and chest clipped as closely as possible.

With standards, the average litter is seven to eight with miniatures four to five, and with toys two to three. Be chary of toy litters claimed to be five or more puppies.

It is up to you to decide where you want the accouchement to take place and to provide a whelping pen or box. The floor should be of wood and the sides should be built up to eliminate drafts. She will let you know a short time before delivery by becoming fidgety and nervous. You will have to watch her closely and encourage her to do her whelping in the place provided, for at the last moment she might decide to have her puppies in a closet or on your new sofa. The floor of the box should contain several layers of newspapers, and you should have plenty of dry cloths available and a pair of dull-point sterilized scissors. Hospital silence should prevail throughout the whelping time. When the first puppy comes, the dam will probably be lying on her side. When the puppy emerges it is securely enclosed in a sack, and when the sack is ejected it is connected with the cord and the afterbirth. As soon as the sack is ejected, she will reach around to bite the cord in order to open up the sack. It is your job to prevent her biting if you can, as they sometimes bite too close to the body and a hernia results. With the scissors cut the cord about two inches away from the puppy's body. Your dog will probably want to eat the afterbirth. This is not harmful but will not do any good either, so if you can prevent it, by all means do so. Thousands of years ago dogs, in their wild state, might have had their location detected and their puppies eaten, and to prevent any odor upon the wind, nature told them to eat the afterbirth.

She will lick the puppies in order to dry them off as quickly as possible, and here you can be of definite help by wiping them off with a dry cloth. The puppies will almost immediately start nursing.

After whelping is completed, pick up all soiled newspapers and put down fresh—cut up but not too fine. As newspaper is absorbent, it is the best for this purpose. After whelping, feed the mother poultry broth or milk at room temperature.

On the fourth or fifth day the tails should be cut and dew claws taken off by a veterinarian. I might mention here that some continental breeders, especially those of the old school, have a deeply rooted prejudice against the removal of dew-claws, because, they claim, it can cause a nervous upset to a highly strung dam. The same prejudice exists in circuses and menageries, when there have been many instances of a bitch killing her litter as soon as she has smelled blood on the puppies. Why she should not do so if the tails alone are cut, nobody knows. Possibly because the dew-claws bleed more profusely than the tails, she gets the impression that her puppies have been maimed or lamed in some way, and so the ancient instinct of destroying wounded or sickly animals is awaked. When there is a deformed or sickly puppy in a litter, particularly one with a split palate that cannot suckle, the mother will nose it away from the rest, and if the puppy does not die she will kill it. However, the dew-claws are one of nature's superfluities, and the dog is better off without them. They catch on plants and roots and can be most painful when allowed to ingrow and curl. They are also in the way for clipping the front feet and do not tend to improve the appearance of the paws and legs.

Make sure that the tail is cut neither too short nor too long. There are various methods for securing the right tail length. Some count the vertebra, others say that twenty-five per cent of the tail should be removed, but the best rule to follow is: For standards, leave about an inch and a quarter of tail; with miniatures, seven-eighths to one inch; and with toys, about three-quarters to seven-eighths. Cut a piece of stiff cardboard to the right size and give it to the veterinarian so he may place it underneath the tail. Naturally, if some of the puppies appear to be large, a little more tail should be left, about one-eighth of an inch, and if there are any that look as though they are going to be skinnies, the tail might be cut a trifle shorter. The tails and the openings left by the removal of the dew claws will heal rapidly with the help of the dam. As the veterinarian hands each puppy back to you to return to the box, it is an excellent idea to check him and make certain that the dew claws have been removed.

On the ninth or tenth day, the pups' eyes will open, and they will be blue in color until about six weeks of age. Then they change to their true color.

At three weeks the nails of the puppies should be cut. They will be clawing at their mother, and although she will not complain, you will do much toward making her comfortable if you make certain the puppies do not scratch her.

At six weeks the puppies should be weaned, but it is best not to wait until this time before getting them accustomed to food other than mother's milk. There are two reasons for this: First, to accustom them gradually to solid food so that there will be no stomach upsets at weaning time; second, the early intake of solid food adds substance to the puppies. So, at four or five weeks, feed the puppies tiny bits of meat in pellet form, or else scrapings of meat. They will lick it off your fingers. They might also be given a small quantity of pablum and milk, and on occasions let them lick some Vitamin E from your fingertips. After they are weaned they may be put on their own diet, which should consist of at least five meals a day.

Long before they are weaned, they should receive daily grooming with brush and a fine comb, and it is imperative that their rears are kept clean and combed out.

At eight weeks of age the puppies should be wormed by a veterinarian. Be most particular in picking up all droppings immediately, for it is a simple thing for puppies to reinfect themselves with worms.

Don't wait until the puppies are sold before making up pedigrees. At two or three weeks of age, application for the registration of the litter should be sent in to the American Kennel Club and the pedigrees prepared showing complete color background.

chapter 7

DISEASES

AND PARASITES

A little learning is a dangerous thing.
POPE

DOGS HAVE THEIR OWN DISEASES JUST AS HUMAN BEINGS do, and as children have mumps, scarlet fever, and influenza, puppies have distemper, worms, skin diseases, and other infections. The most important precautionary measure in the bringing up of a puppy is cleanliness. This applies to his living conditions, food, drink, and other habits. The condition of a poodle's skin, coat, and eyes is usually an accurate reflection of his general health. In most nonparasitic diseases of the skin, faulty nutrition may be blamed, although there are other contributing causes such as lack of circulation, faulty metabolism, emotional imbalance, and, of course, in overheated apartments and houses, temperature is an important factor.

DANDRUFF

This is a dryness of the outside layer of skin, characterized by small particles of skin falling off in scales. It can usually be remedied at home by a daily brushing with a whalebone or bristle brush and moderate exercise in the sun and air and regular elimination. With some types of dogs, this condition is remedied by a mild application of olive oil to the skin, but this might be inadvisable with a poodle because of the texture of his coat. A teaspoonful of wheat-germ oil or olive oil mixed in with the main daily meal is recommended.

DERMATITIS

This is an advanced form of dandruff with either a slight or serious inflammation of the skin. If serious, it is accompanied by pimples or blisters. It may be the result of the causes mentioned previously or of internal parasites, excessive exposure to the sun, or bites of insects. The important thing is to prevent itching, as this brings constant scratching which will spread and aggravate the condition. A mild hand lotion containing menthol and lanolin will be helpful and will usually clear up the situation if it is not too bad. Balanced meals are most essential. If the condition persists, the dog should be examined by a veterinarian.

ECZEMA

This is probably the most overworked word in dogdom, for almost any type of skin condition is referred to as eczema. True eczema involves intense itching of the skin, inflammation, and loss of hair. There are two types: dry eczema, which is the aggravated stage of dermatitis not previously attended to; and wet eczema, which is the acute form. Among the contributing causes of this condition are a deficiency of proteins, fats, carbohydrates, and minerals, or an allergy to one of these. The veterinarian will have to determine the proper food balances. Eczema may also be caused by the use of a strong disinfectant, soaps, dirt, weeds, or insect bites.

Age has no relation to eczema, and it can attack any part of the dog's body. It is found most frequently between the toes, under the neck, or at the base of the tail. It generally starts with itching and with the hair falling from certain spots. This is followed by a red skin, and then a scaly condition. It is important not to confuse the periodic shedding of some breeds with eczema. In eczema only small portions of the skin are involved in the beginning.

It is most important to determine the cause, for if a cure is to be effected the cause must be destroyed. A vigorous daily brushing of the coat and skin is essential, together with the utmost cleanliness in the dog's sleeping quarters. The dog must be prevented from scratching himself as much as possible, since scratching can easily become a habit. Lotions applied should contain benzyl which mildly anesthetizes the skin and thus minimizes itching. A veterinarian should be consulted for specific remedies. Treatment should begin immediately so that the spread of the disease can be checked quickly.

RINGWORM

This is a fungus infection and should not be considered trivial. It is a disease communicable to man. It is characterized by circular lesions on the skin which gradually increase in size. When the scab is removed there is a bleeding on the surface of the skin. Immediate attention must be given this disease for if allowed to go unchecked it may take many weeks to cure. The hair should be clipped around the lesions, all scabs removed, and tincture of iodine applied. The hair and scabs should not be touched by human hands but should be immediately burned. Sleeping quarters should be disinfected.

MANGE

This is a serious contagious skin disease caused by tiny mites. There are two types of mange, sarcoptic and demodectic—the names derived from the two different types of mites. In the sarcoptic type the female burrows into the skin and lays her eggs. The male lives on the surface of the skin under the crust or scab. The disease makes its appearance first around the head, eyes, and nose, and occasionally on the abdomen. Unless immediate treatment is given, the entire body may become diseased. The itching is intense and the scratching will be violent. Treatment is somewhat difficult as the mites, being under the skin, are not easily reachable. As the disease is sometimes confused with other skin afflictions, it is necessary to have a microscopic examination of skin scrapings before positive diagnosis can be made. There are various efficacious treatments for this disease, but all of them involve a clipping and shaving of the entire body before dipping and other treatment.

Demodectic mange, called red mange, is exceedingly difficult to cure. The mite lives in the hair follicle and sometimes in the skin glands. The disease develops slowly, and one indication of it is round bare spots from which the hair has fallen. In its primary stage it is found around the face. As the disease progresses, itching becomes pronounced and small hard pimples resembling blisters occur. There is a distinct thickening of the skin, which becomes dry and gradually takes on a copper color. As soon as any symptoms appear a veterinarian should be consulted and microscopic examination should be made. Following this, the body will be shaved and specific remedies applied. Sleeping and other quarters frequented by the dog are bound to be infected, therefore disinfection is necessary in order to prevent re-infection.

TICKS

There are over eight different species of ticks in the United States, and all of them are dog parasites. The most pestiferous types are the American dog tick and the brown dog tick. The former is probably the most widely distributed and its bite may carry Rocky Mountain spotted fever if the tick is infected. A dog running through grass in an infected area may pick up several hundred ticks during the course of the day. The male never grows large but the female becomes greatly enlarged by feeding on blood. When she is completely gorged, she falls off the dog, lays her eggs, and dies. She will lay an average of forty-five hundred eggs in a mass. These ticks are usually picked up in the open.

The brown dog tick is the troublesome pest of city dogs. It is the cosmopolitan type and thrives in warm houses and apartments. It can live for two years without feeding, usually snuggling behind a baseboard. If it can find a dog as a host, the female, after feeding, drops off and lays her eggs, and the offspring can live a year without food.

In warm houses and apartments the female usually crawls into the baseboard or under the edge of the rug to lay the eggs.

If ticks are found on the dog they should be taken off only with tweezers and dropped into kerosene. The strictest of sanitary precautions should be taken and fingers should not touch the tick. The dog should be rinsed or dipped twice a week in a solution that contains a sufficient percentage of hydrogenated rotenone and rotenoids or a United States Government approved type of non-toxic chlordane. Unfortunately many of the commercial types of "tick killer" solutions do not possess all the killing qualities advertised. A tick is just about the most difficult of all pests to kill, and even with those remedies known to be effective it requires from twenty-four to forty-eight hours to kill. Do not be deceived by the apparent immobilization of the tick. The solution immediately paralyzes the legs—death to follow later, depending upon the age of the tick, its resistance, etc. The removal of ticks from dogs is not too difficult a task, but if the brown dog tick becomes a tenant in your home, prepare for an extended campaign. The baseboards, cracks, and crevices should be sprayed, and also under the rug. Continue as long as the pest is observed. More important, the sleeping quarters of the dogs should be thoroughly sprayed. Some of these sprays, if non-toxic, may safely be sprayed on the leg coat of the dog as a repellent.

LICE

There are two types of lice that affect dogs, the blood-sucking, and the type that lives on the skin and hair. Scratching and rubbing is less pronounced with lice than with fleas. A mild inflammation of the skin caused partly by lice and the scratching are the main symptoms. If your dog scratches a great deal and you do not find fleas, he should be checked for lice. The dog may be examined under a magnifying glass, or better yet in the sunlight. Lice are usually found in the tips of the ears. Ordinarily the situation will not be serious if treated promptly, and many effective remedies are available. In long-haired dogs it is most important that the ears be kept out of the food dish, as particles of food on the ear tips will attract lice. In treating a dog for lice, have him stand on a large sheet of paper and comb him out with a fine flea comb. After this treatment burn the paper and then dip him in an insecticide solution guaranteed to kill lice. It may take two or three treatments for a thorough cure. If the dog has a heavy infestation his body may have to be clipped.

WORMS

The most effective way to control worms is sanitation in the kennels. The elimination of fleas and lice will do much toward stamping out tapeworms. Promiscuous worming is to be guarded against. Practically all of the chemicals used for the elimination or destruction of worms are poisonous and toxic. The very best professional advice should be sought, and specific microscopic diagnosis undertaken. Dosages for worming should be administered by a veterinarian or under his specific instruction and guidance. The amount of drugs to be used has to be computed carefully on the basis of the weight and age of the dog.

TAPEWORMS

There are various types and sub-types of tapeworm. Generally, it is a long, flat worm composed of many segments and smaller at the head than at the tail. Each of these segments can separate and cause infection to other dogs. The flea finds the egg of the worm in the dog's hair or in a kennel and eats the egg. The egg hatches within the flea and the dog swallows the flea. Some types of tapeworm require two hosts. Symptoms of infection are loss of appetite, dull coat or eyes, and skin eruptions. The dog may become nervous and may lose weight notwithstanding the intake of nourishing food.

HOOKWORMS

The hookworm is a species of roundworm most damaging to puppies. It is from one-half to one inch in length and may be acquired through the mouth or the skin, or infection may occur even before birth. It has a mouth equipped with hooks that bury themselves and remain fast to the mucous membrane of the intestine. Early infection may be detected by digestive upsets and by streaks of blood in the feces. The infection is usually in the small intestine. The worm is destructive as it withdraws blood with its bite, which results in general debility and may result in an anemic condition. Loss of weight ensues and there is a marked depressive attitude. Positive diagnosis can be made only through microscopic examination of the stool.

WHIPWORMS

These worms are from two to three inches in length and derive their name from their resemblance to small whips. The worms attach themselves to the mucous membrane of the blind gut, and their habitat makes it most difficult to remove them. Symptoms include unexplained fits, nervousness, and bloody diarrhea. The worms sometimes can be eliminated by rectal treatment with medication.

ASCARIDS

These worms are found in the large intestine and are from one inch to nine inches in length. Infections can occur before birth. They are exceedingly injurious in that they may obstruct the intestine. Their presence is sometimes indicated by a sweetish odor of the breath, general listlessness, and a bloated stomach.

DISTEMPER

This is a highly contagious disease caused by a virus. It occurs in puppies from three weeks to a year of age, but has been observed in older dogs. It practically never occurs while puppies are unweaned. Puppies having a lack of condition, or eating an unbalanced diet, or living in an unsanitary place and lacking moderate exercise are particularly susceptible to this disease. It is the most dangerous disease dogs have, is very apt to be fatal, and is infectious even before any of the symptoms are observable. Infection may spread by direct or indirect contact. Anti-canine distemper protection, cleanliness, and proper care with particular regard to nutrition are important in guarding against this disease.

Symptoms are varied. The early ones are so faint as not to admit of quick detection. General listlessness and a rise in temperature are usually the first indications, followed by a lack of appetite. Later on a mucous discharge from the eyes and nose and respiratory and nervous disturbances will result. Notwithstanding high temperature, there will be a shivering accompained by a dry nose and a slight dry cough, and there may be diarrhea. It may be likened to influenza in human beings. Owing to the introduction of bacterial invaders, other symptoms might include chest, stomach, and nerve disorders. The disease, if detected in its early stages, and treated with anti-canine distemper serum, penicillin, and sulfa drugs as indicated, should not prove fatal. All-abiding care must be given the puppy, which means clean, comfortable, warm and dry quarters and attentive nursing. Small amounts of easily digested food should be force-fed, and the eyes and nose should be washed daily with a mild antiseptic solution such as boric acid. Directions given by your veterinarian should be followed closely.

A vast amount of research work has been done in connection with the prevention of this scourge. It is now considered absolutely safe to give a puppy, at an age from six weeks to three months, his "temporary" shots. These provide temporary immunization. They are injections in proper doses of anti-canine-distemper serum, homologously prepared from the blood of dogs hyper-immunized against the distemper virus. These temporary shots can be given safely at three-week intervals.

Permanent immunization may be given a puppy over three months of age by one of several methods; leave the choice to your veterinarian, who has a tried and proven method. The usual methods are: 1) The injection of three canine distemper vaccines at two- to three-week intervals. 2) The administration of vaccine followed by attenuated live virus at two-week intervals. 3) The administration of anti-canine-distemper serum and live virus.

No vaccination is fool-proof, but if the puppy has an attack of distemper the treatments will be milder and the chances of recovery greater. The dog to be vaccinated must be free of parasites and rickets and have general all-around health.

chapter 8

P O O D L E   P R O F I L E S

The idol is the measure of the worshipper.
LOWELL

THROUGH THE CENTURIES THE NAMES OF DOGS HAVE come down to us as the friends and esteemed companions of famous people—purebreds, mongrels, sleevedogs, almost everything that barks and wags its tail. Among the royal dogs there were, of course, the white standard poodles of Louis XIV. Charles II bred and accumulated the little snub-nosed spaniels that bear his name. Napoleon made the Samoyede his choice, and the stuffed relic of his favorite dog holds a place of honor in the Museum des Invalides, a stone's throw from the tomb of his master.

Then, as now, dogs were prominent in the world of arts, letters, and the drama; Byron's lines to his St. Bernard stand out in a nostalgic epitaph tinged, perhaps, with a faint trace of bitterness: "Praise, which would be unmeaning flattery if it were inscribed over human ashes, is but the just tribute to the memory of Boatswain—a dog." Sir Walter Scott went in for Dandie Dinmonts; Burns had a collie. In our day poodles have found their place in the hearts of writers. The late Gertrude Stein, Alexander Woollcott, and Booth Tarkington were among the first to write about theirs.

The joy of owning a poodle, whether you bred it yourself, bought it, or acquired it in your Christmas stocking, knows no bounds. All growing puppies are fascinating to watch, and the character of the poodle develops rapidly; its intelligence is such that it learns at an early age. All dogs reflect the personality of their owners, and it is up to you to set a good example to yours at all times. They like articulateness, punctuality, common sense, and, above all, good manners. There is no dog more capable of adapting himself to your ways than the poodle. Their faces mirror their minds in a way that wraps itself around your heartstrings in a double bowline that nothing can sever except death. They are humorous and inclined to practical joking in a gentlemanly sort of way, while their smile is something to remember always.

Quentin Reynolds has written: "I was never a poodle lover because it seemed to me that most poodles were artificially and consciously cute. They learned a trick or two and at the slightest provocation would perform, then sit back with a sense of spurious modesty and wait for the inevitable applause. There was never any spontaneity or gaiety in their performance. If you teach a four-year-old child a poem, allow her to recite it once, and then are foolish enough to applaud, you have a child ham on your hands. That heady applause is something she wants to enjoy again and again, and any time three people gather in your house the little brat will just stand there waiting until you coax (?) her to perform. This is very annoying to friends of the family, and often the only remedy is the application of a dull, blunt instrument to the head of the precocious child.

"I have often felt that way about poodles. For years I have heard the same old story of how smart poodles are. People who own poodles discuss their qualities to the point of nausea. They often end up by saying 'Suzette (or Koko or Minette or CloClo) is much smarter than anyone in the family,' which is probably an understatement.

"Finally a poodle came to my house to live and she turned out to be a living refutation of every sickening thing I had ever heard or learned about the breed. We call our little monster Folly, which is a good one-word description of her. She is a toy poodle (and was the runt of her litter). At one year she weighs four pounds. Although her pedigree shows good blood lines, there must have been a bit of carelessness somewhere in her family background, for Folly's left front leg is half an inch shorter than her right front leg, and her ears are an inch longer than those of the standard toy poodle. She refuses contemptuously to learn any tricks and is definitely not consciously (or unconsciously) cute. Folly is a complete extrovert, a gay abandoned clown whose size often evokes such remarks as, 'What a darling little doggie.' When Folly hears such a remark she is apt as not to go into the corner and become sick. Folly is practically unbreakable. She leaps blithely off chairs and beds and has the resiliency of a cat.

"Poodle lovers usually drag their dogs out as soon as company arrives, and the applause-conscious dogs go through their repertoire of tricks with eager alacrity. There is nothing of the ham in Folly. She merely yawns when people come to the house unless she happens to know and like them. She rather resents any outsiders and she sulks until they are gone. Strangely enough, she likes children, perhaps because they don't patronize her. Children amuse her, and she likes anyone who amuses her. Most poodles insist upon being performers; Folly occasionally likes to be a spectator.

"Folly is at her best late at night. Then the house is hers. She tears all over the place, growling menacingly at some sinister shadow, yelping joyously if she has managed to knock over a box of cigarettes or a porcelain knickknack. Folly never whines or begs for attention the way most poodles do. She doesn't woo you; if you want her friendship you must woo her, and not with conventional candy, jewel, or sable wrap, but with your sincere attention.

"The street is a jungle to Folly, but one in which she likes to hunt. She is completely unafraid and will propose combat to a boxer, a bulldog, or a horse. She seems to dislike other poodles. In our living room there is a full-length mirror. At least once a day Folly, seeing another poodle in the mirror, barks furiously and dashes toward the image with teeth bared. It is the only time Folly really gets angry.

"Folly is a confirmed television fan and will sit for hours watching the screen. She especially enjoyed the Westminster Dog Show at Madison Square Garden until they showed the class of poodles. She slunk away then in disgust, perhaps at the thought of being related to any of those dressed up floosies with their fancy hairdos. Folly has a Dutch cut and she sometimes looks as ridiculous as any of them, but happily she doesn't know this. I think her resentment at the dog she sees in the mirror is caused by the way the dog's hair is clipped. If she ever discovers that dog is herself, I expect trouble."

Ilka Chase gives her poodle Mr. Puffle a sparkling profile: "Having been asked what the poodle means to me, my reflections at first ran in orthodox channels. I, too, have read books and articles and heard lectures. I, too, know about man's best friend; loyalty and loving companionship sound fine, I thought to myself, that's just what I'll say, but when I sat down at the typewriter my fingers stuck. 'Why don't you,' they said (they're a chatty bunch), 'why don't you tell the truth?' Well, I like to keep on good terms with my fingers, being dependent on them and all, so I thought to myself, why don't I indeed? High time somebody told the truth about dogs, poodles in particular. I don't speak for other poodles, but what mine means to me is constant distraction.

"I sit down to work, and my poodle sits down on the couch. My husband and I are better disciplined. We sit on the floor. He sits there surrounded by sani-bones, balls with bells in them, solid balls, chocolate-flavored rubber bones with bells in them, odd objects made out of burlap, and a round stuffed thing with ears like a rabbit which squeaks. Watching him divert himself with this paraphernalia is distracting, prevents me from getting a full morning's work done. The answer to that is simple, you say. Put him out of the room. But once he's out the distraction is accentuated, since he merely keeps scratching on the door till he is let in again; two and a half to three minutes. Man's best friend, my eye!"

Esmé Davis (Esmé of Paris), who has nine poodles, speaks from experience: "My penchant for poodles began some years ago when I was breeding French bulldogs and Bostons. I had just lost a favorite pet, and was haunting the dog shows and kennels in search of another, when a sympathetic friend offered me a miniature poodle. For the first time in my life I refused the gift of a dog. Somehow I had formed a misguided idea of the breed that contrasted unfavorably with the short-coated and moon-faced dogs I had specialized in; in fact, I visualized a drawing-room ornament with a beribboned top-knot and complicated grooming problems. But one day, while visiting a friend's kennels, I came across a small white poodle sitting forlornly in a cage, and the expression of his dark almond shaped eyes and sensitive face fascinated me.

"Of course I bought him, regardless of points or anything else, and he taught me many things. First, that poodles, be they standards, miniatures, or toys, are gentlemen to their backbones. Not only do they possess a keen sense of humor and an almost human intelligence, but are undoubtedly mind readers of the first water. They are sportingly inclined, and most of them have a distinct social complex. They like to get around and meet the right people, and they love cars and excitement; furthermore, they are aristocrats and inclined to be critical about their owner's behavior, especially in public. The poodle is also the great lover of the dog world, presumably an inheritance from his French training, and I ought to know—I've got nine now.

"Anyway, to describe their beauty and elegance seems superfluous, since they have become the fashion in a big way with the introduction of the Dutch cut or modern boxy clip that has replaced the classic English saddle and Continental styles except for show purposes. But whichever is preferred, the job of grooming, brushing, etc., loses its tediousness when one realizes their candid vanity and the satisfaction they derive from looking their best, to say nothing of the boost it gives one's personal pride and the joy of owning a poodle."

And Mignon G. Eberhart writes: "I have never owned a poodle but poodles have owned me. I am but a slave. I have washed poodles, brushed, combed, and beribboned poodles; I have walked enough miles, tugging at the end of a poodle's leash, to make in round numbers a dent in the national debt. I have roused in the dead of night to fling myself into clothes and off trains, poodle under arm, and trudged up and down, uttering low cries of encouragement while anxiously watching for the porter's signal to leap back on the train again. The New York-San Francisco jaunt is difficult; stops are rare and brief. On the New York-Florida trek you sally forth somewhere in the deeps of Georgia about four in the morning. But the Chicago-New York trip is wonderful; Toledo after dinner, Harmon before breakfast—blessed Harmon, where engines shuffle around for ten minutes and there is a long concrete platform.

"I need not add that porters greet me with delight—not because of me or poodle; a poodle is not an inexpensive luxury.

"However, I am not alone in abject slavery; once, when crossing a desert in the middle of the summer, the air-cooling system went off. I suffered and so did my secretary. But the poodle? Oh, no. I found my secretary putting ice bags on his head. Then there was the time we went to live on a naval base; the poodle needed a haircut, and eventually a very tough sergeant in the Marines offered to trim the poodle—and did. I know the sergeant was very tough, because the poodle, up to then gentle and amiable, went straight from the sergeant to pick a furious battle with a bigger dog. Obviously a case of influence; leave it to the Marines.

"I have also thrust my trembling hands into dog fights, than which there is simply nothing in the world more terrifying.

"In short, I like poodles. Monsieur Beaucaire, a small brown figure with a shocking pink tongue and very bright eyes, is waiting now for the typewriter to stop, when he will turn into a tornado in pantaloons. The extreme sensitiveness of the poodle is one of his charms; his gaiety, his loving heart, his uncanny intelligence. As I said, I like poodles."

There is no doubt that the poodle has become the most fashionable dog in the world today. Adaptable, elegant, gay, and charming, they fit into the modern social scene just as they did a hundred years ago, and the list of their enraptured owners would fill Debrett. Beautiful Mrs. John Kelly, née Brenda Frazier (who has tiny gray toys), Mrs. Irving Berlin, Mrs. Edward D. Madden, Mrs. James M. Austin, of dog-show fame, and Mrs. James Lowell Oakes, Jr.—their name is legion.

Mrs. Oakes tells us: "Poodles are fun! I have had more fun with my toy Tillie than I ever had with any other breed. People who do not care for dogs have gone mad about my Miss Matilda, as they cannot help falling in love with a dog who possesses such a charming personality. Of course, she is spoiled, but upon my firm insistence she is going to school and learning obedience training. There she will learn to sit down and to walk by my side and all the other commands, but I do not want her ever to lose her love of people. I do not want her to stop jumping up on the back of our love seat or barking at our bar until someone gives her a drink of water out of a cocktail glass. And I do not want her to stop wrapping up her favorite toy or biscuit in a piece of paper to put away for a surprise finding later on, at which she works as hard as if she were wrapping up a Christmas present. She has never been anything but a joy since we bought her. She has motored with us more than six thousand miles, and if it is chilly, she will snuggle inside my fur coat. A smart traveler, she prefers to sleep in dresser drawers in hotels at night. I cannot bear to think of her ever growing old or ever losing her joie de vivre."

In the world of the stage the poodle has come to stay. There, too, he has found a natural element for his many-faceted nature, from the chorus of Billy Rose's Diamond Horseshoe to the glittering stars of the Broadway stage. Helen Hayes, Fredric March, Ruth Chatterton, Estelle Winwood, Eddie Dowling, and Harold Lang are poodle owners. In the wonderland of the movies Claudette Colbert, Sam Wanamaker, Joan Bennett, Joan Crawford, Elizabeth Taylor, and others join in the chorus of praise for poodles. And where could we find a

more generous outpouring than the following comments from Cobina Wright, Sr., who says: *"Poodles are people.* Never for a moment have I ever considered any of my pets as being dogs, because every poodle I have ever owned or known has always had his—or her—own personality, just like a human being.

"Perhaps that is why I am partial to poodles above all other breeds. They are intelligent, lovable, and have an individual charm. They are quick to learn—I even trained one of mine to sing—they are devoted, and they are never cross or ugly.

"By all means give him the attention you would to a child, and you'll be rewarded with the most faithful love and adoring attention you could ever expect from your dearest loved one."

Then, Joan Crawford's description of her poodle, Cliquot: "Cliquot is used to attention and of course he gets a lot of it at home from my four children, Christina, Christopher, and the twins, Cynthia and Cathy.

"He liked attention at the studio, too. When I'm working in a scene and have no time for him he wanders over to other sets until he finds someone who is free to make over him. I guess he just likes the spotlight.

"He must have a sixth sense. When I'm sleeping he is a model of deportment. The minute I'm up and awake, he knows it and sets up a howl until he is allowed in the room to wish me good morning. No matter what part of the house he's in, he knows when I'm awake and will receive him. Like all poodles, he's a wonderful companion and pet."

The matter of the humanization of the poodles has its perils as well as its humorous aspects. Bert Lytell's black standard has a passion for carrying home ice cream after dining out with his master. It has reached the point where, if he should go home without a package, he will stop every stranger carrying one and insist on taking it home with him. Marion S. Dresser will testify under oath that her handsome brown standard, Michel, frequently ambles into the Colony Restaurant and orders for himself a glass of sherry with egg mixed in. Gracie Allen was told about this and asked if her poodle could top that. Gracie said, "What's unusual about that? I frequently like an egg mixed in with my sherry."

Gladys and Richard Diaz, of Pasadena, California, take their black standard Topper to ball games, where he avidly follows the course of the ball and barks loudly in unison with the cheers when a home run is hit. He eats popcorn and hot dogs, goes to movies, dives off the diving board into the swimming pool, and floats around the pool on a rubber raft, as if he were a producer.

Koko, who belongs to the I. W. Magoverns of New York, has a penchant for wheeling baby carriages. The moment he spies one he gets up on his hind legs and takes over. He will walk solemnly and grandly for blocks, pushing the carriage with the solemn countenance of a proud father. Curiously enough, in going through revolving doors, he confuses the horizontal bar with that of a baby carriage handle and delights in pushing round-'n-round.

Cherie, owned by Dick Rahns of Cabazon, California, contradicts every theory that poodles prefer the companionship of people to that of another animal, including a poodle. Cherie's companion is a pet rooster with whom she pals around constantly. In the yard is a Navy hammock, and when Cherie feels languid she will crawl in and dangle her hind legs over the side like a drunken sailor.

Suzie, owned by Mr. and Mrs. Charles N. Crittenton of Greenwich, Connecticut, is a scavenger and saves beer cans. Beau-Beau, Jo Stafford's miniature, insists on attending college classes with her, while Pierette, owned by the M. Johnsons of New York, spurns all meat and will eat only cantaloupe and bananas.

My Perky (Celia of Puttencove) has the snoopy habit of opening each and every package that enters the house. Size is no deterrent; any package, from one of bobby pins to a mattress, is set upon with all the possessive eagerness of a gold digger. She is readily forgiven, however, because her devotion and responsiveness are more than one is entitled to. Her innate charm is truly more than one can bear, and her intelligence, gentility, and decency cause one to pause at times and view humans with a skeptical eye.

And speaking of skepticism, Colonel John V. Grombach says: "I have owned but two kinds of pets and am therefore partial to both. Parrots and poodles are the best and most pleasant companions that man can have, and far more dependable than women. Neither a parrot nor a poodle will ever walk out on you, and neither will ever insist on talking back to you or having that last word; more important, neither can throw things.

"The parrot, and even to a greater degree the poodle, is a creature with a sharp but delicate sense of humor. The poodle is a robust, Gallic individualist with a heart all out of proportion to his body. His love is all-consuming, constant, and unselfish. His rare bark of warning or special joy is both useful and satisfying. His intelligence is positively scintillating in the canine world and even the seal cannot match him as an all-round vaudeville performer.

"The poodle is human, in fact far more so than many of his two-legged friends. My wife has a brown, Wickette, a shapely, stylish sexy number from Paris, who, I am sure, from the very start had designs on me from the many little things she did. She was certain she was like everyone else except perhaps for a lack of speech until one day she unfortunately happened to see herself in a mirror.

"The shock was one of the saddest things I have ever seen. The memory of that fleeting moment of supreme disappointment is one of my bitterest experiences. 'What,' dolefully wondered my brown love, 'I am not a human after all but only a four-footed woolly little thing —a dog?' The dog as revealed in the mirror barked a heart-rending cry, took another look at the mirror to be certain she was actually not like all her dearest friends, and then, yes, tears—real watery tears formed in the two saddest human eyes I have ever seen."

Columnist H. I. Phillips, reading a news item to the effect that a dog had left an estate of forty-five dollars which would go to his master who had put it in a bank for him, thought that a poodle might draw up a will as follows: "Being of sound mind (except in the matter of cats, squirrels, and sudden noises at night), I declare this to be my last will and testament:

1. To my master I bequeath the forty-five dollars. It is nothing to a dog, but I understand that to human beings it is of consequence. I once chewed a dollar bill. It tasted awful. It didn't, in fact, even smell good. I hope there will be no fighting over the forty-five dollars. I know no dog will stage a contest for it, but I understand it is surprising what some people will do for that much money.

2. I leave all my jewelry to my master and missus. My idea of what constitutes jewelry is sketchy and I am not certain of what the word means. However, if it means what I hope it means, I herewith list it as follows:

    a. The string of precious memories of the relationship between a pooch and his owners.
    b. The bright, warm, round spot which moved around the house in such a mysterious way and which, if I remember, was called

the sun. (I always liked to lie in it, and to me it seemed a pretty priceless possession. I may have hogged it a lot. I am sorry and want them to have it now.)

c. The big bright star which I used to see gleaming in the skies from the foot of the bed where I often slept.

d. The 44-karat memories of long winter nights in the lap of those who loved me, and of long summer nights at their feet on the front porch.

e. The rubber ball, playbone, and chewed socks which gave me the feeling I guess a millionaire gets with money and automobiles.

3. To be divided share and share alike between my master and my missus, I bequeath all other personal property, including swell recollections of long walks together and rompings in the park; also, share and share alike, my love, devotion, and loyalty.

4. I leave nothing to the brown and white pooch which lived next door, having made ample provision for its happiness during my lifetime.

5. I cut off completely the airedale four houses north. (It has been running around with a police dog.)

6. I give fair warning that if anybody or any pooch attempts to break this will I shall return to haunt them, and if they have never been haunted by the ghost of a dog they do not know what a sleepless night is.

7. I am sorry for the hole in the Turkish rug under the dining-room table which I chewed only a few days ago and which may be discovered any minute. (Use some of the forty-five dollars to fix it up.)"

Although poodles are subject to caricature, manufacturers take them seriously. Almost any article of commerce can be found today in illustration of this. Scarves, socks, and hats are manufactured with poodles' hair, and there is some talk of its being utilized in other types of wearing apparel. Suffice it to say, there is nothing new under the sun. The Reverend W. Bingley, who wrote his comprehensive (for that time) treatise *British Quadrupeds* in 1804, with an introduction to the female reader that he "must remark, that every indelicate subject is scrupulously excluded," mentioned in his work that he knew the owner of a poodle who cut off the coat "twice in the year; and each fleece is found sufficient to be manufactured into hats . . . worth about twelve shillings each." In 1899 Lee wrote of sending four pounds of wool shaven from his poodle to Scotland to have it spun. He found the yarn silky, though hard of texture, and had socks made from it, commenting after wearing them that the socks were "harsh and whiskery" but judged they would be all right to wear in the English climate! Such poodle apparel may very well have been responsible for the old Cockney music-hall ditty:

> Sister Susie's sewing socks for soldiers,
> Such saucy soft short socks our shy young
> Sister Susie sews;
>
> The soldiers send epistles—say they'd
> sooner step in thistles,
> Than the saucy soft short socks for
> soldiers Sister Susie sews.

For the ultrasophisticated there are even poodle chaise longues advertised by a well-known house of elegance. They are copied from one used in the days of the Regency, which was "made for an English lady who wanted his chaise next to hers . . . a general custom among Regency belles," as the ad puts it. The couch runs into three figures, "unfortunately without the poodle," the ad explains apologetically.

Yes, " 'tis a merry world, my masters"—in the marketplace one can buy dresses, coats, lapel pins, tablecloths, napkins, coasters, lamp bases, drinking glasses, stationery, earrings, cocktail bags, belts, radiator caps for cars, tiles, ash trays, greeting cards, umbrellas, and canes—all with a poodle motif or decoration. Tin Pan Alley has picked up the beat and turned it into two songs, "Let Me Play with Your Poodle" and "Serenade to a Poodle," all in glorification of the breed.

Of all the qualities of poodles, their unchanging affection and gratitude are most endearing. You are the generous dispenser of all good things, and they are quick to see and appreciate your kindness, yet sensitive when scolded or ignored. They do expect you to appreciate the little things they do for you, and they are right, these scholars and jesters.

APPENDIX

THE IDEAL POODLE

THE POODLE CLUB OF AMERICA HAS RULED THAT THE description and standard of points of the ideal poodle may be set forth as follows. This standard was approved by the American Kennel Club on February 14, 1940.

1. GENERAL APPEARANCE, CARRIAGE AND CONDITION
That of a very active, intelligent, smart and elegant-looking dog, squarely built, well proportioned, and carrying himself proudly. Properly clipped in the traditional fashion and carefully groomed, the poodle has about him an air of distinction and dignity peculiar to himself.

2. HEAD AND EXPRESSION
   a. Skull—should be slightly full and moderately peaked with a slight stop. Cheekbones and muscles flat. Eyes set far enough apart to indicate ample brain capacity.

   b. Muzzle—long, straight and fine, but strong without lippiness. The chin definite enough to preclude snipiness. Teeth white, strong, and level. Nose sharp with well-defined nostrils.

   c. Eyes—oval shape, very dark, full of fire and intelligence.

   d. Ears—set low and hanging close to the head. The leather long, wide, and heavily feathered; when drawn forward almost reaches the nose.

3. NECK
Well proportioned, strong, and long enough to admit of the head being carried high and with dignity. Skin snug at throat.

4. SHOULDERS
Strong, muscular, angulated at the point of the shoulder and the elbow joint, sloping well back.

5. BODY
The chest deep and moderately wide. The ribs well sprung and braced up. The back short, strong, and very slightly hollowed, with the loins broad and muscular. (Bitches may be slightly longer in back than dogs.)

6. TAIL
Set on rather high, docked, and carried gaily. Never curled or carried over the back.

7. LEGS
The forelegs straight from shoulders with plenty of bone and muscle. Hindlegs very muscular, stifles well bent, and hocks well let down. Hindquarters well developed with the second thigh showing both width and muscle.

8. FEET
Rather small and of good oval shape. Toes well arched and close, pads thick and hard.

9. COAT
    a. Quality—*Curly Poodles*: Very profuse, of harsh texture, even length, frizzy or curly, not at all open. *Corded Poodles:* Very thick, hanging in tight even cords.

    b. Clip—Clipping either in traditional Continental or English Saddle style is correct. In the Continental clip, the hindquarters are shaved, with pompoms on hips (optional), and in the English Saddle clip, the hindquarters are covered with a short blanket of hair. In both these clips the rest of the body must be left in full coat. The face, feet, legs, and tail must be shaved, leaving bracelets on all four legs, and a pompom at the end of the tail. The topknot and feather on the ears must be long and profuse, so as not to lose the very essential poodle expression. A dog under a year old may be shown with the coat long except the face, feet, and base of tail, which should be shaved. Any poodle clipped in any style other than the above mentioned shall be disqualified from the show ring.

10. COLOR
Any solid color. All but the brown have black noses, lips, and eyelids. The browns and apricots may have liver noses and dark amber eyes. In all colors toenails either black or the same color as the dog.

11. GAIT
A straight forward trot with light springy action. Head and tail carried high.

12. SIZE
The Standard Poodle is fifteen inches or over at the shoulder.

13. DESCRIPTION AND STANDARD OF POINTS OF THE IDEAL MINIATURE POODLE
a. Same as standard poodle.

b. Size—under fifteen inches at shoulders.

c. Value of points—same as standard poodle.

d. So long as the dog is definitely a miniature, diminutiveness is only the deciding factor when all other points are equal; soundness and activity are every whit as necessary in a miniature as they are in a standard poodle, and as these traits can be seen only when the dog is in action, it is imperative that miniatures be moved in the ring as fully and decidedly as standard poodles.

14. DESCRIPTION AND STANDARD OF POINTS OF THE IDEAL TOY POODLE
a. Same as standard poodle.

b. Size—ten inches and under at shoulders.

c. Value of points—same as standard poodle.

d. So long as the dog is definitely a toy, diminutiveness is only the deciding factor when all other points are equal; soundness and activity are every whit as necessary in a toy as they are in a standard poodle, and as these traits can be seen only when the dog is in action, it is imperative that toys be moved in the ring as fully and decidedly as standard poodles.

15. VALUE OF POINTS

General appearance, carriage and condition	20
Head, ears, eyes, and expression	20
Neck and shoulders	10
Body and tail	15
Legs and feet	10
Coat, color and texture	15
Gait	10

16.   MAJOR FAULTS
      Bad mouth—either undershot or overshot
      Cow hocks.
      Flat or spread feet, thin pads.
      Very light eyes.
      Excessive shyness.

17.   DISQUALIFICATIONS
      Particolors.
      Unorthodox clip.

RECOGNIZED BREEDS OF DOGS

BY SPECIAL ACT BY THE NEW YORK STATE LEGISLATURE, the American Kennel Club was granted a charter in order to enact and enforce uniform rules and regulations with respect to, among other things, the registration of dogs. Pursuant to its authority, it has officially recognized as distinct breeds the dogs listed below as purebred and thus eligible for registration in the Stud Book of the American Kennel Club. These breeds are divided by groups.

HOUNDS

Afghan Hounds
Basenjis
Basset Hounds
Beagles
Bloodhounds
Borzois
Coonhounds (Black and Tan)
Dachshunds
Deerhounds (Scottish)
Foxhounds (American)
Foxhounds (English)
Greyhounds
Harriers
Norwegian Elkhounds
Otter Hounds
Salukis
Whippets
Wolfhounds (Irish)

TOYS

Affenpinschers
Chihuahuas
English Toy Spaniels
Griffons (Brussels)
Italian Greyhounds
Japanese Spaniels
Maltese
Mexican Hairless
Papillons
Pekingese

Pinschers (Miniatures)
Pomeranians
Poodles (Toy)
Pugs
Toy Manchester Terriers
Yorkshire Terriers

SPORTING DOGS

Griffons (Wirehaired Pointing)
Pointers
Pointers (German Shorthaired)
Retrievers (Chesapeake Bay)
Retrievers (Curly-coated)
Retrievers (Flat-coated)
Retrievers (Golden)
Retrievers (Labrador)
Setters (English)
Setters (Gordon)
Setters (Irish)
Spaniels (American Water)
Spaniels (Brittany)
Spaniels (Clumber)
Spaniels (Cocker)
Spaniels (English Cocker)
Spaniels (English Springer)
Spaniels (Field)
Spaniels (Irish Water)
Spaniels (Sussex)
Spaniels (Welsh Springer)
Weimaraners

TERRIERS

Airedale Terriers
Bedlington Terriers
Border Terriers
Bull Terriers
Cairn Terriers
Dandie Dinmont Terriers
Fox Terriers
Irish Terriers
Kerry Blue Terriers

Lakeland Terriers
Lhasa Apsos
Manchester Terriers
Norwich Terriers
Schnauzers (Miniature)
Scottish Terriers
Sealyham Terriers
Skye Terriers
Staffordshire Terriers
Welsh Terriers
West Highland White Terriers

WORKING DOGS

Alaskan Malemutes
Belgian Sheepdogs
Bernese Mountain Dogs
Bouvier des Flandres
Boxers
Briards
Bull-Mastiffs
Collies
Doberman Pinschers
Eskimos
German Shepherd Dogs
Great Danes
Great Pyrénées
Komondorok
Kuvaszok
Mastiffs
Newfoundlands
Old English Sheepdogs
Pulik
Rottweilers
Samoyedes
Schnauzers (Giant)
Schnauzers (Standard)
Shetland Sheepdogs
Siberian Huskies
St. Bernards
Welsh Gorgis (Cardigan)
Welsh Gorgis (Pembroke)

NON-SPORTING DOGS

Boston Terriers
Bulldogs
Chow-Chows
Dalmatians

French Bulldogs
Keeshonden
Poodles (Miniature)
Poodles (Standard)
Schipperkes

THE INTERNATIONAL SET

Belgium (Flemish)	Poedel	Lithuania	Kudius
Belgium (Wallon)	Caniche	Netherlands	Poedel
Czechoslovakia	Pudl	Norway	Puudel
Denmark	Pudel	Poland	Pudel
Estonia	Puudel	Portugal	Cao d'Agua
Finland	Villa Koira	Siam	Ma Khon Pui
France	Caniche	Spain	Perro de Lanas
Germany	Pudel	Sweden	Pudel
Greece	Thasytrichon	Syria	Kalb Poodle
Iceland	Puddel Hunder	Union of South	
Italy	Barbone	Africa	Hond
		United States	Poodle
		U.S.S.R.	Pudel
		Yugoslavia	Pudel

I N D E X